Paul's Prayers

Aligning the Righteous with God

Wendy Bowen

DEDICATION

To Jesus, for teaching me how to pray.

CONTENTS

PAUL'S PRAYERS

Introduction

THE PURPOSE OF MY INSTRUCTION IS THAT ALL
BELIEVERS WOULD BE FILLED WITH LOVE THAT
COMES FROM A PURE HEART, A CLEAR CONSCIENCE,
AND GENUINE FAITH.
– THE APOSTLE PAUL, 1 TIMOTHY 1:5 NLT

A little over five years ago, I had a mid-prayer-life crisis. The Lord had asked me to give away everything that I owned and to live by prayer and obedience to His voice without asking man for anything that I needed. I was already well into a walk of living in this manner with no home of my own, no car, no money, no income, and most of the people in my life thinking that I had lost my mind. I was fully dependent on answered prayer for even my most basic needs. While these needs were always met, sometimes even supernaturally so, it did not seem like anything else in my life was going my way or the way that I thought God's will should look like.

I cried out to God in tearful exasperation, saying, "Well, clearly I don't know how to pray! I'm not praying anymore! You're going to have to teach me!" Up to this point, I had learned to pray in the way that the Church teaches—promises from Scripture mixed with faith and expectation…and *voila!* something exceedingly and abundantly beyond what we dreamed of should happen. Not to mention, I had seen many miracles on my path already, so I was fully assured that God was with me and leading me. Plus, I suppose that I presumed that my radical and self-sacrificial obedience to God's voice should have procured even more victory, success, and abundance for me. Instead, He was leading me on a narrow and difficult path. Go figure.

Please hear me. I was genuinely trying to pray what I believed to be God's will, but I did not understand His ways. My perceptions were immature and my desires were carnal, even in the midst of definitive surrender and obedience. It was as if the Lord was saying to me, as He did to Peter when Peter refused to believe that it was God's will for Him to suffer, "Get behind me, Satan! You are a hindrance to me. You have on your mind the ways of man and not of God." (see Matthew 16:23) Needless to say, my life and my prayers were all being sifted, pruned, and crucified.

I did not hold to my vow of prayerlessness for very long but that was mostly because I was involved in so many prayer groups. This said, these meetings began to cause me agony in my heart because the Holy Spirit within me did not bear witness to the things that people were praying. During this time and in these meetings, the Holy Spirit would reveal to me what was going to happen in the situations that we prayed about (and it would come to pass exactly as the Holy Spirit said), but what was prayed and what the Holy Spirit said were oftentimes as different as night and day. I sat silently, not correcting anyone, being taught by the Holy Spirit about the ways and will of God, and occasionally being mocked or ridiculed for my silence.

About a year after my crisis of prayer and crying out to the Lord, the Lord told me to stop attending prayer meetings and to stop praying for people with the exception of praying into any prophetic insight or promptings to prayer that He spoke to me directly. As is often the way of God, something has to die before it can be resurrected. My prayer life laid dormant for almost a full year before the Lord resurrected it with the prayers of the Apostle Paul. This certainly does not make me a theological expert on the topic and I'm not trying to be one. However, what I discovered in Paul's prayers is the heart of God, a mirror to the Lord's Prayer, a deep abiding in the ways of the Holy Spirit, and an effective way of praying prayers that are affirmed in heaven and confirmed in the earth.

PAUL'S PRAYERS

While there are many volumes that could be written on the many different forms of prayer, the Apostle Paul gives us an excellent and irrefutable example of how to pray and what prayer is really all about. His prayers are found interspersed in his letters to the churches which encompass most of the New Testament as we know it today. Even though they were prayed from Paul's heart for believers in the churches back then, they are inspired by the Holy Spirit and are accurate in accordance with the will of God. Arguably, they are the prayers that Paul would be praying for us today if he were on earth, and they very well may be the prayers that he is praying for us from heaven when he has time in between worship sessions.

Paul's prayers are primarily centered on drawing believers into a deep comprehension of all that Christ has accomplished for us through His death and resurrection and a dynamic and intimate relationship with God through the Holy Spirit. Therefore, Chapters 1 and 2 of this study lay a foundation of the Gospel of Jesus Christ and the simplicity of pure devotion to Him. The remaining chapters present a compilation of Paul's prayers for believers, for laborers, and for the lost, immersing us in Paul's way of calling and praying believers into the highest heights of wisdom and spiritual understanding and the deepest depths of love and submission to God and His purposes. The prayer teachings and example of Jesus and some reference to Old Testament prayers are also woven into this study in order to demonstrate the remarkable consistency of God and to confirm Paul's approach to prayer for God's New Covenant people. This said, I do not feel the need to over-scrutinize or dissect Paul's prayers ad nauseam but, rather, to present them in a way so as to allow them to speak for themselves and so that the heart and purpose of God is magnified.

THE AIM OF OUR CHARGE IS LOVE

Unfortunately, too often in the Church, believers seek to use prayer as a method of turning God into their servant rather than the other way around. Too many prayer teachings focus on how to get God to give us what we want rather than listening to God so that we can give Him what He wants. It seems habitual in the Church for prayer to be focused on asking God to bless our plans rather than offering ourselves freely to align with God's will and His plans. Prayer is too frequently focused on our circumstances and problems, the nations and politics, the lost and asking

3

God to change those who aggravate us, or anyone or anything other than the things that God may be seeking to prune, sift, change, or purify in our own hearts. All of these things cause us to feel like we are diligently communicating with God and serving Him when, all the while, we are not actually receiving His love for us as His children, allowing Him to renew our minds as His holy ones, or laying down our lives for Him as His servants.

In contrast, the Apostle Paul said that *the aim of our charge is love.* (1 Timothy 1:5) This *love* in Greek is *agape,* meaning *charity, unselfishness, unconditional benevolence, and unceasing good will* regardless of circumstances and whether or not this love is returned. Indeed, this is the purpose of the Christian life: to be conformed to the image of the Son of God, Jesus Christ, who embodied perfect *agape* as the exact image of His Father, God, who is *love.* (Romans 8:29; Colossians 1:15; Hebrews 1:3; 1 John 4:8) Jesus knew and trusted in the love and goodness of His Father and willingly submitted Himself to God's will for His life, no matter the cost and no matter what man did to Him so that God's eternal plan of redemption could be fulfilled. (Isaiah 53:7; 1 Peter 2:23; Hebrews 12:3; Philippians 2:1-8) Accordingly, the aim of this teaching is for you to know the unfathomable love of God for you in Christ and the sufficiency of His sacrifice on your behalf so that you willingly lay down your life, your dreams, your plans, your preferences, your opinions, and your way of doing things in order to walk in *agape* love, trust, and obedience to God and His plans for your life.

If I haven't lost your interest yet, then I invite you to join me in studying Paul's Prayers: Aligning the Righteous with God. May God the Father draw you into the depths of His love, may Christ the Son be your constant comfort and companion, and may the Holy Spirit give you strength to endure and be transformed into the image of perfect love.

CHAPTER ONE

THE GOSPEL

FOR I AM NOT ASHAMED OF THE GOSPEL, BECAUSE
IT IS THE POWER OF GOD THAT BRINGS SALVATION
TO EVERYONE WHO BELIEVES: FIRST TO THE JEW,
THEN TO THE GENTILE. FOR IN THE GOSPEL THE
RIGHTEOUSNESS OF GOD IS REVEALED--A
RIGHTEOUSNESS THAT IS BY FAITH FROM FIRST TO
LAST, JUST AS IT IS WRITTEN: "THE RIGHTEOUS WILL
LIVE BY FAITH."
– THE APOSTLE PAUL, ROMANS 1:16-17

The Apostle Paul said that the mindset of the spiritually mature is to live in such a way that we continually move forward towards living out the fullness of all that Jesus attained for us through His life, death, resurrection, and ascension. In line with this, Paul's prayers summon followers of Jesus into a deeper understanding of the Good News and what it means for our lives here on earth. Therefore, before we examine Paul's prayers, let us take a moment to review the Gospel. It is important for us to grasp some level of understanding of how God did what He did in the spiritual transaction that He worked in Christ so that we can know of and more readily receive the benefits that are freely available to us as we trust in Him. Knowing these things to the deepest extent possible is what strengthens us to live our lives by God's indwelling resurrection power, hold firmly with confident expectation that God will fulfill all of His promises of life and blessing for us, and move forward to spiritual maturity in Christ.

This Chapter gets a little technical but I will try to keep it as simple and brief as possible without neglecting anything significant. This said, because Paul's prayers repeatedly emphasize the things that we will cover here, you may find yourself returning to this Chapter as we move through this study. There is also a quick-reference chart at the end of this Chapter to reveal plainly what Jesus has done for us.

A BRIEF SYNOPSIS OF THE GOOD NEWS

Jesus Christ was born of a virgin by the power of the Holy Spirit into the lineage of King David of Israel. Israel was the only nation on earth that had a covenant relationship with the one and only true God, the Creator of Heaven and earth, and they were earnestly awaiting the Messiah or King that God promised them who would establish His Kingdom and set things right in the world. They were also the only people on earth with God's Law and standard of justice and righteousness which, if upheld, led to blessing, eternal life of fellowship with God, and inheriting all creation. Unfortunately, no man on earth has ever been able to live up to this standard of purity and godliness. As a consequence, all of mankind since the first man Adam has been separated from God because of falling short of perfect obedience to God's instructions. That is, until Jesus came along.

Because Jesus was conceived by the power of the Holy Spirit, He was born with the divine nature of God, His Father. He was simultaneously fully God and fully man, the exact image of His Father, and a full demonstration and incarnation of God in the flesh. Because Jesus followed the inclinations of His indwelling divine nature and not those of His flesh, He lived His life completely without sin according to the Law of God. His motives and actions always stemmed from God's perfect love, mercy, and justice so that He was completely righteous by God's standard. Additionally, God confirmed Jesus as His Son and the promised Messiah with power from Heaven by enabling Jesus to supernaturally heal the sick, cast out demons, raise the dead, and work various other miracles, signs, and wonders.

However, instead of being accepted as a righteous man, the Son of God, the Messiah of Israel, and the Lord and King of all the earth, the religious leaders of Israel and the governmental authorities of this world unanimously mocked, rejected, and sentenced Jesus to death like a criminal, acting on behalf of all people. Jesus was whipped and scourged, and His blood was shed, until He was ultimately nailed to a cross and crucified until He was dead. He was buried in a tomb and thought to be thoroughly defeated. In fact, for three days, it appeared that Jesus was the world's biggest failure and that He had horribly deceived all of His followers.

But God, with resurrection power by His Spirit, raised Jesus from the dead on the third day before His body had experienced decay. Jesus walked out of the grave in an imperishable resurrection body, having conquered death. For forty days, He revealed Himself to His disciples as proof that He is, indeed, alive from the dead and the Son of God who fulfills the prophecies concerning the Messiah of Israel.

After forty days of resurrection appearances, Jesus ascended in the clouds from Jerusalem to His Father in Heaven, where He is now seated at the right hand of God, the position of all power and authority over all creation. At the appointed time, He is coming back to judge the living and the dead, avenge all evil, abolish death, establish total dominion, restore all things, and hand the Kingdom back to His Father as He fulfills the remaining prophecies concerning Himself.

Until He returns, after He ascended to Heaven, Jesus poured out the Holy Spirit into the hearts of all of us who believe in Him so that God's divine nature now dwells in us by faith. This means that we have Christ inside of us just like Jesus had God inside of Him when He was on the earth in the flesh. With Christ in us, we are empowered to live like Jesus lived, to love like He loved, and do the things that He did while we are still here on earth in these bodies. We are citizens of heaven and children of God, serving as His ambassadors with a message of His Kingdom, His goodness, and His love.

A SPIRITUAL TRANSACTION

God worked a marvelous masterpiece of redemption through Jesus' life, death, resurrection, and ascension. God established a New Covenant for His people and created a New Covenant people for Himself. A covenant is a legally binding agreement between two or more parties that is typically sealed with blood to obligate the parties to obey the terms of the covenant at the expense of their own blood or life. Up to this point, the only people on earth who had a binding covenant with God were the people of Israel. We know of this as the Old Covenant, or the Law, which was given to them by Moses and specified the details of how to maintain their special relationship with God.

Originally, God created mankind to know Him and to be the object of His love, the recipient of His blessing, and the ruler over all that He created. Unfortunately the first man, Adam, decided it was more important to have knowledge of good and evil than to obey God's instructions. When he ate from the wrong tree, he forfeited mankind's position of favor with God. Many generations later, God chose one man, Abraham, out of all the people of the earth to reinstate access to His love and blessing for all mankind through faith. Abraham believed God and eventually had a miraculously born son, named Isaac, who inherited God's blessing to Abraham. Isaac had a son named Jacob, who inherited the blessing of God, and whose name God changed to Israel. Israel had twelve sons who became the twelve tribes of Israel and eventually became the nation of Israel. After Moses led them out of Egypt through the parted waters of the Red Sea, God gave them the Law, or Old Covenant. This said, God also promised the people of Israel a New Covenant through which God would allow everyone to know Him directly and to receive all of His blessings. When Jesus came, He fulfilled the Old Covenant and shed His blood to seal and ratify the New Covenant and put it into effect. This means that He is legally bound by His own blood to fulfill the terms of the New Covenant to everyone who is included in it.

> *Jeremiah 31:33-34 - "This is the covenant I will make with the people of Israel after that time," declares the LORD. "I will put my law in their minds and write it on their hearts. I will be their God, and they will be my people. No longer will they teach their neighbor, or say to one another, 'Know the LORD,' because they will all know me, from the least of them to the greatest," declares the LORD. "For I will forgive their wickedness and will remember their sins no more." (see also Hebrews 8:12)*

> *Jeremiah 32:40-41 - I will make an everlasting covenant with them: I will never stop doing good to them, and I will inspire*

them to fear me, so that they will never turn away from me. I will
rejoice in doing them good and will assuredly plant them in this
land with all my heart and soul.

As a predecessor and foreshadow of the New Covenant, God's Old
Covenant required believers and new converts to be circumcised in their
flesh and to subject themselves to God's Law in order to be included with
His people. But now in the New Covenant, believers and new converts
are spiritually circumcised in their hearts by faith. When we place our
faith in Jesus and are submerged into the waters of baptism, we
symbolically demonstrate that our old self has entered into Christ's
death. As we come up out of the waters, our old self is rolled away in
spiritual circumcision and we emerge as a whole new person. We are
born again in Christ as God's children and become His New Covenant
people so that we can willingly give our lives to the obedience which
comes from faith.

> *Colossians 2:11-13 - In him you were also circumcised with a*
> *circumcision not performed by human hands. Your whole self*
> *ruled by the flesh was put off when you were circumcised by*
> *Christ, having been buried with him in baptism, in which you*
> *were also raised with him through your faith in the working of*
> *God, who raised him from the dead. When you were dead in*
> *your sins and in the uncircumcision of your flesh, God made you*
> *alive with Christ. He forgave us all our sins,*

Through the New Covenant, we who believe Jesus have unhindered,
perpetual, direct access to God as our loving Heavenly Father. Because
Jesus fulfilled the specifications of God for having a relationship with
Him, we are not subject to any rules and regulations or to the Old
Covenant and we are no longer separated from God or penalized by Him
for our imperfections and errors. Our past, present, and future sins have
been completely forgiven and our position of favor with God has been
restored to the condition that it was in before Adam made the wrong
choice. Therefore, we can know God for ourselves and we are able to
freely receive all of God's benefits and blessings according to our faith. In
fact, in the New Covenant, because of what Jesus has done for us, we are
dearly loved by God and it gives Him great pleasure to bless us!

THE BLOOD OF JESUS & BROKEN BODY OF CHRIST

Through His shed blood and broken body, Jesus paid the price for all of our sins, including anything that we have done or not done, and gave us access to God's presence forever. Here's how He did it:

Under God's regulations, only one man, the High Priest, was allowed to enter into His presence behind the veil in the Temple, in the one place on earth where God had chosen to dwell, and this was only once per year on the Day of Atonement after specific blood sacrifices of bulls, sheep, and goats had been offered. (see Leviticus 16; Deuteronomy 12) Anyone else who attempted to enter into God's presence at any other time instantly dropped dead. Needless to say, even the one man who was allowed to go behind the veil at the appointed time did so with fear that he might not make it out alive.

The reason that sacrifices had to be offered before any man could enter into God's presence is because sin, dating all the way back to Adam's first error, creates a blemish and a debt that causes all people to be unfit to enter into God's holy presence. Think of it this way. Hypothetically, let's say that a king here on earth necessitates that certain prerequisites are met for anyone seeking an audience with Him. Anyone who does not satisfy the requirements of the king is turned away because they are not suitable to be in the presence of his majesty. How much more should this be true for the King and Creator of all the earth! Fortunately, God is good enough to give explicit details of His requirements and how they can be satisfied. The standard of God for entering into His presence is purity and holiness. The only way to attain this is through the shedding of blood of an unblemished sacrifice of atonement. (see Leviticus 17:11) Moreover, the sacrifice must be equal in worth to the cost of the error according to God's value system in order to reconcile accounts and pay the debt in full. Sin is only forgiven through a blood sacrifice which meets God's specifications and it is only through the forgiveness of sin that anyone can have right standing with God and enter into His presence.

However, because Jesus lived His life without sin, He had no need of a blood sacrifice and could reside in God's presence at all times. Not only that, but His own blood and body qualified by God's standard as an unblemished sacrifice of atonement for the sins of all mankind. The life of a human has far more value than that of any animal in God's sight and the life of the Son of God has inestimable value. Knowing this, even though He was the Son of God, totally innocent, and could have stopped His trial, beating, and crucifixion at any moment, Jesus willingly laid His life down in order to fulfill God's eternal plan. (see Hebrews 10:5-9; 1 Peter 1:18-20; Revelation 13:8)

> *Isaiah 52:14-15a, 53:4-7, 10 - Just as there were many who were appalled at him-- his appearance was so disfigured beyond that of any human being and his form marred beyond human likeness-- so he will sprinkle many nations, and kings will shut their mouths because of him... Surely he took up our pain and bore our suffering, yet we considered him punished by God, stricken by him, and afflicted. But he was pierced for our transgressions, he was crushed for our iniquities; the punishment that brought us peace was on him, and by his wounds we are healed. We all, like sheep, have gone astray, each of us has turned to our own way; and the LORD has laid on him the iniquity of us all. He was oppressed and afflicted, yet he did not open his mouth; he was led like a lamb to the slaughter, and as a sheep before its shearers is silent, so he did not open his mouth. ... Yet it was the LORD's will to crush him and cause him to suffer, and though the LORD makes his life an offering for sin, he will see his offspring and prolong his days, and the will of the LORD will prosper in his hand. (quoted as fulfilled by Christ in 1 Peter 2:24)*

This willing and obedient sacrifice of His beloved Son has infinite value in God's sight, more than millions upon millions of offerings of lambs, goats, bulls, birds, grain, oil, new wine, and all the silver and gold in the world. This means that we can be completely confident that Jesus' sacrifice was totally sufficient payment in full for all of our faults and failures and the countless ways that we have fallen short of God's perfect standard. We have been purified and made holy.

> *Hebrews 10:10, 14 - And by that will, we have been made holy through the sacrifice of the body of Jesus Christ once for all. ... For by one sacrifice he has made perfect forever those who are*

being made holy.

Through the shed blood of Jesus, our sins have been paid for in full. This means that we are completely forgiven, without blemish, continually clean, and purified from all sin. We have perpetual right standing with God as if we had never sinned and have been made holy and perfect in God's sight. For this reason, we can have a clear conscience before God because our right standing with Him no longer has anything to do with our own performance or measuring up to His standard because it is now completely secure through our faith in Jesus' blood that was shed for us.

Romans 3:25a - God presented Christ as a sacrifice of atonement, through the shedding of his blood--to be received by faith.

Ephesians 1:7 - In him we have redemption through his blood, the forgiveness of sins, in accordance with the riches of God's grace.

Hebrews 9:14 - How much more, then, will the blood of Christ, who through the eternal Spirit offered himself unblemished to God, cleanse our consciences from acts that lead to death, so that we may serve the living God!

1John 1:7 - But if we walk in the light, as he is in the light, we have fellowship with one another, and the blood of Jesus, his Son, purifies us from all sin.

Through the offering of His body, Jesus made a way for everyone who trusts in Him to enter into the presence of God. Before taking His final breath, Jesus cried out, "IT IS FINISHED!" At that very same moment, the veil in the Old Covenant Temple was torn from top to bottom. This means that now, instead of the Old Covenant specifications of one man having access to God one time per year in one designated place on earth, the New Covenant grants direct access to God's presence every day of the year in every place where believers are present.

Colossians 1:19-22 - For God was pleased to have all his fullness dwell in him, and through him to reconcile to himself all things, whether things on earth or things in heaven, by making peace through his blood, shed on the cross. Once you were alienated from God and were enemies in your minds because of your evil behavior. But now he has reconciled you by Christ's physical body through death to present you holy in his sight, without blemish and free from accusation.

Hebrews 10:19-22 - Therefore, brothers and sisters, since we have confidence to enter the Most Holy Place by the blood of Jesus, by a new and living way opened for us through the curtain, that is, his body, and since we have a great priest over the house of God, let us draw near to God with a sincere heart and with the full assurance that faith brings, having our hearts sprinkled to cleanse us from a guilty conscience and having our bodies washed with pure water.

All of this is to say that through the shed blood and broken body of Jesus, God's righteous standard of purity and holiness has been met in full and we can enter into God's presence with total confidence that we are completely accepted by Him. Because of this, we can know God for ourselves.

THE DEATH & BURIAL OF CHRIST

Through His death and burial, Jesus put to death our sinful nature which stems all the way back to our first ancestor, Adam, nullified all of our personal advantages and disadvantages, and set us free from the curse of the Law. Here's how He did it.

While Jesus was on the cross, we were being crucified with Him. When He died, we died with Him. When He was buried, we were buried. Every descendant of Adam was included in His crucifixion, death, and burial. Just to be clear, this includes you, me, and every person ever born throughout the entire course of history.

Galatians 2:20 - I have been crucified with Christ and I no longer live, but Christ lives in me. The life I now live in the body, I live by faith in the Son of God, who loved me and gave himself for me.

2 Corinthians 5:14 - For Christ's love compels us, because we are convinced that one died for all, and therefore all died. (see also

John 12:32)

Galatians 6:14 - May I never boast except in the cross of our Lord Jesus Christ, through which the world has been crucified to me, and I to the world.

Through His death, Jesus allowed all punishment for sin and every accusation against all of mankind to be unleashed on Himself. The curse of the Law from the Old Covenant outlines God's schedule of retribution for all forms of disobedience and these penalties includes all forms of sickness and demonic oppression, death, and exile from God's presence. (for the curse of the Law, see Deuteronomy 28 and Leviticus 26) At the cross, the record of charges against us for everything that we have done or not done or will ever do to deserve God's punishment were remembered by God. His wrath and vengeance were completely poured out until we all died with Jesus. Jesus died and was fully confirmed as dead before they took Him down from the cross and buried Him. He gave Himself up to the devil, who holds the power of death, and for an appointed time, the ruler of the kingdom of darkness overpowered the light of the world. (see Luke 22:53)

Needless to say, the death penalty is the ultimate punishment. But consider carefully that the death penalty also brings to an end the possibility of the offender being able to commit further offenses. Not to mention that in any righteous court, there is no double jeopardy, meaning that we cannot be tried and condemned again for crimes that have already been punished. Accordingly, because we are regarded by God as dead in Christ's death and the death penalty has already been satisfied in full, we have no further possibility of warranting God's punishment. This also means that the curse of the Law is rendered void against us. God remembered our sins, past, present, and future on the cross of Christ and now He remembers them no more.

Romans 8:33 - Who will bring any charge against those whom God has chosen? It is God who justifies.

Galatians 3:13 - Christ redeemed us from the curse of the law by becoming a curse for us, for it is written: "Cursed is everyone who is hung on a pole."

Colossians 2:14-15 - Having canceled the charge of our legal indebtedness, which stood against us and condemned us; he has taken it away, nailing it to the cross. And having disarmed the powers and authorities, he made a public spectacle of them, triumphing over them by the cross.

Hebrews 8:12-13 - For I will forgive their wickedness and will remember their sins no more." By calling this covenant "new," he has made the first one obsolete; and what is obsolete and outdated will soon disappear.

This also means that, through our inclusion in Jesus' death, God removed every hindrance of our humanity and nullified every genetic and generational limitation. Nothing about our race, gender, family history, nationality, or personality has any impact on God's love for us because the nature that we inherited from our first ancestor Adam is as good as dead in God's sight. Moreover, everything that our sinful nature produces, including all of our fleshly lusts, impurities, worldliness, selfishness, and depravity have no right to rule over us or to reverse our right standing with God because we ourselves are as good as dead in His sight. Even our circumstances and our personal advantages or disadvantages have no influence on God's plan for us or blessings towards us. Think of it this way. Dead people don't have anything going for them and they are far too dead to be disadvantaged by anything. In Christ's death, we are dead.

Romans 6:3-7 - Or don't you know that all of us who were baptized into Christ Jesus were baptized into his death? We were therefore buried with him through baptism into death in order that, just as Christ was raised from the dead through the glory of the Father, we too may live a new life. For if we have been united with him in a death like his, we will certainly also be united with him in a resurrection like his. For we know that our old self was crucified with him so that the body ruled by sin might be done away with, that we should no longer be slaves to sin-- because anyone who has died has been set free from sin.

Colossians 3:3 - For you died, and your life is now hidden with

Christ in God.

Being dead and buried with Christ is exactly what we have going for us! There is no longer anything from our human nature that can hinder us from receiving God's love and blessings, even our inclination towards perpetual sin, error, and wrong choices. Hallelujah!

THE RESURRECTION & ASCENSION OF GOD'S SON

Through His resurrection and ascension, Jesus raised up everyone who believes in Him to new and everlasting life, delivered us from the power of death, hell, and the grave for all time, and caused us to become citizens of heaven. Here's how He did it.

In Jesus' death and burial, it truly seemed that death and the grave had triumphed as the Son of God descended into the place prepared for the devil and his angels. But on the third day, God resurrected His beloved Son, Jesus Christ, out of the grave in an imperishable body. Jesus was begotten again (or born again) by God and was delivered out of the domain of the evil one. The power of sin, the curse, death, the devil, and the powers of darkness were overcome and neutralized by the resurrection power of God. The gates of Hell did not prevail against the Son of God in His death, and everyone who believes Him was with Him. (see Matthew 16:18) In this, God fulfilled His promise of eternal life to His perfectly righteous Son.

Through our inclusion in His resurrection, God created a New Covenant people for Himself. We have been born again (or begotten by God) as God's children. This means that the devil and all of his workers have no right to harm us because powers of darkness have no authority over our lives as children of the light. We never have to fear death (or anything else) again because we have been given everlasting life.

> *Colossians 1:13-14 - For he has rescued us from the dominion of darkness and brought us into the kingdom of the Son he loves, in whom we have redemption, the forgiveness of sins.*

> *John 5:24 - "Very truly I tell you, whoever hears my word and believes him who sent me has eternal life and will not be judged but has crossed over from death to life.*

Hebrews 2:14-15 - Since the children have flesh and blood, He too shared in their humanity so that by His death He might break the power of him who holds the power of death--that is, the devil-- and free those who all their lives were held in slavery by their fear of death.

1 Peter 1:3-5 - Praise be to the God and Father of our Lord Jesus Christ! In his great mercy he has given us new birth into a living hope through the resurrection of Jesus Christ from the dead, and into an inheritance that can never perish, spoil or fade. This inheritance is kept in heaven for you, who through faith are shielded by God's power until the coming of the salvation that is ready to be revealed in the last time.

As if that is not enough, when Christ ascended to Heaven after forty days of resurrection appearances, we also ascended with Him. Consequently, spiritually speaking, we are no longer subject to the limitations of this world because we are seated in Christ at the right hand of God.

Ephesians 2:4-6 - But because of his great love for us, God, who is rich in mercy, made us alive with Christ even when we were dead in transgressions--it is by grace you have been saved. And God raised us up with Christ and seated us with him in the heavenly realms in Christ Jesus

Ephesians 1:3 - Praise be to the God and Father of our Lord Jesus Christ, who has blessed us in the heavenly realms with every spiritual blessing in Christ.

Yes, even while we are here in the imperfections of our flesh and the brokenness of this dark world, we are truly and totally accepted by God as perfect and we live in the throne room of heaven. In Christ, we have been restored to a place of authority over all creation. Hallelujah!

A New Creation in Christ

Through His life, death, burial, resurrection, and ascension, the Old Covenant has been fulfilled, the New Covenant has been established. God created a whole new people group, a new type of humanity for Himself to be His New Covenant people who can know Him, be the object of His affection, recipients of His blessings, and who have authority to rule over all creation. (see Ephesians 2:10, 14-16) Nothing about our old self matters anymore because this new humanity includes Jew and Gentile from every nation, tribe, and tongue. (see Revelation 5:9; Galatians 3:28; Colossians 3:11) Though our faith in Jesus, we are totally pure vessels who are able to hold the divine nature of God. He no longer dwells in a Temple made by human hands but now has chosen to dwell in our hearts as we trust in His Son.

> *2 Corinthians 5:17 - Therefore, if anyone is in Christ, the new creation has come: The old has gone, the new is here!*

> *Hebrews 9:15 - For this reason Christ is the mediator of a new covenant, that those who are called may receive the promised eternal inheritance--now that he has died as a ransom to set them free from the sins committed under the first covenant.*

Accordingly, after Jesus ascended to heaven, He poured out the Holy Spirit into the hearts of all who believe in Him. (see Acts 2:33) The nature of God and the very Spirit of Christ now dwell inside of all of us who place our faith in Jesus. The Holy Spirit is what gives us power and ability to live as children of God and as a totally new creation in Christ.

> *John 14:23 - Jesus replied, "Anyone who loves me will obey my teaching. My Father will love them, and we will come to them and make our home with them.*

> *Colossians 1:27 - To them God has chosen to make known among the Gentiles the glorious riches of this mystery, which is Christ in you, the hope of glory.*

> *2 Peter 1:3-4 - His divine power has given us everything we need for a godly life through our knowledge of him who called us by his own glory and goodness. Through these he has given us his very great and precious promises, so that through them you may participate in the divine nature, having escaped the corruption in the world caused by evil desires.*

We who believe the Gospel are a heavenly people in earthly tents of flesh and a resurrected people in un-resurrected bodies. We have been reborn as children of God so that we can live the way that Jesus lived when He was on the earth in the flesh. We can literally do the things that He did in the way that He did them by the power of God and as the Holy Spirit guides and empowers us.

John 3:5-8 - Jesus answered, "Very truly I tell you, no one can enter the kingdom of God unless they are born of water and the Spirit. Flesh gives birth to flesh, but the Spirit gives birth to spirit. You should not be surprised at my saying, 'You must be born again.' The wind blows wherever it pleases. You hear its sound, but you cannot tell where it comes from or where it is going. So it is with everyone born of the Spirit."

Romans 8:14 - For those who are led by the Spirit of God are the children of God.

Luke 6:40 - The student is not above the teacher, but everyone who is fully trained will be like their teacher.

1 John 3:9 - No one who is born of God will continue to sin, because God's seed remains in them; they cannot go on sinning, because they have been born of God.

By the power of the Holy Spirit within us, we can live lives of purity and holiness to reveal God's good nature and love. As the Holy Spirit comes upon us, we are empowered to proclaim the Gospel of the Kingdom of Heaven and exalt the name of Jesus, and we can expect God to confirm the name of His Son with miracles, signs, and wonders. In fact, He sends us out to do exactly that.

Matthew 28:18-20 - Then Jesus came to them and said, "All authority in heaven and on earth has been given to me. Therefore go and make disciples of all nations, baptizing them in the name of the Father and of the Son and of the Holy Spirit, and teaching them to obey everything I have commanded you. And surely I am with you always, to the very end of the age."

John 14:12-14 - Very truly I tell you, whoever believes in me will do the works I have been doing, and they will do even greater things than these, because I am going to the Father. And I will do

19

whatever you ask in my name, so that the Father may be glorified in the Son. You may ask me for anything in my name, and I will do it.

Mark 16:17-18 - And these signs will accompany those who believe: In my name they will drive out demons; they will speak in new tongues; they will pick up snakes with their hands; and when they drink deadly poison, it will not hurt them at all; they will place their hands on sick people, and they will get well."

The more that we believe the Gospel and receive the great love of God for us through all of its benefits, the more we become free to love others the way that Jesus loves us. This is how our own lives are transformed until we walk in the fullness of perfect *agape* love.

PRESSING ON TO MATURITY

If you're not there yet, take heart. You can start today by believing that Jesus is Lord and that God raised Him from the dead. (see Romans 10:9-11) Through your faith in the Gospel of Jesus Christ, the old you is gone and the new you has come. You can know God personally for yourself, receive His love and blessings, and have authority in the earth as a child of its Creator. The only thing that matters for any of us now is to live for Christ so that we may manifest the fullness of all that He has accomplished for us.

This was the way that the Apostle Paul described his mindset and approach to the life of faith as a follower of Jesus.

Philippians 3:10-17 - I want to know Christ--yes, to know the power of his resurrection and participation in his sufferings, becoming like him in his death, and so, somehow, attaining to the resurrection from the dead. Not that I have already obtained all this, or have already arrived at my goal, but I press on to take hold of that for which Christ Jesus took hold of me. Brothers and sisters, I do not consider myself yet to have taken hold of it. But one thing I do: Forgetting what is behind and straining toward what is ahead, I press on toward the goal to win the prize for which God has called me heavenward in Christ Jesus. All of us, then, who are mature should take such a view of things. And if on some point you think differently, that too God will make clear to you. Only let us live up to what we have already attained. Join together in following my example, brothers and sisters, and just as you have us as a model, keep your eyes on those who live as we do.

So, one day at a time, keeping our eyes on Jesus and our ears attuned to the whisper of the Holy Spirit, let us follow Paul's example and press on to spiritual maturity. May God be glorified as we trust in His Son and reveal His love to the world.

PRAYER OF SALVATION

If you have never really understood what Jesus did for us through His death and resurrection or if you desire to be refreshed in your journey with the Lord then pray this simple prayer from your heart.

God, I come to you in the name of Jesus.
I am a sinner and I believe that Jesus is my Savior.
I believe that Jesus is Lord and that You raised Him from the dead.
Wash me with His blood that was shed for me so that I can be clean.
I receive your forgiveness and I forgive those who have offended me.
Fill me with your Holy Spirit and teach me how to love like Jesus.
Amen

See transformation chart on the next page.

The Old You	Set Free by Jesus' Shed Blood & Broken Body Death & Burial Resurrection & Ascension	New Creation
TRANSFORMED THROUGH FAITH IN THE GOSPEL		
Nature of Sin Descended from Adam	Anything that you were born with or into. For example: Race, nationality, tribe, gender, genes, height, age, family patterns, selfishness, depravity, vanity.	**Divine Nature** The Holy Spirit Born Again in Resurrection
Acts of Sin Trespasses Iniquities	Anything done by you, including thoughts and motives. For example: Lying, cheating, moral failures, addictions, lusts, sexual immorality, pride, slander, covetousness, hatred.	**Acts of Righteousness** Purity, Holiness Spiritual Fruit
Curse Afflictions Exile from God	Any limitation on your ability to receive blessing. For example: Lack, defeat, inability to get ahead, sickness, weakness, miscarriages, subjugation, broken relationships.	**Blessings** Victory, Health Access to God
Kingdom of Darkness False Spirituality Religion	Any involvement that you have had with works of the devil. For example: The occult, idol worship, consulting spirits and the dead, curses, witchcraft, vows, astrology, karma, religious legalism, wisdom of man, tradition.	**Kingdom of Heaven** Light of the World Total Freedom
Personal Attributes Advantages Disadvantages	Anything that you have going for you or against you. For example: Birthrights, experiences, wealth/poverty, marital status, successes/failures, strengths/weaknesses, education, the way that you were raised.	**Child of God** Living Hope Eternal Inheritance

CHAPTER TWO

THE SIMPLICITY
OF DEVOTION

I AM JEALOUS FOR YOU WITH A GODLY JEALOUSY. I
PROMISED YOU TO ONE HUSBAND, TO CHRIST, SO
THAT I MIGHT PRESENT YOU AS A PURE VIRGIN TO
HIM. BUT I AM AFRAID THAT JUST AS EVE WAS
DECEIVED BY THE SERPENT'S CUNNING, YOUR
MINDS MAY SOMEHOW BE LED ASTRAY FROM YOUR
SINCERE AND PURE DEVOTION TO CHRIST.
– THE APOSTLE PAUL, 2 CORINTHIANS 11:2-3

God has made it very simple for us to freely receive His love and all the benefits that the Gospel includes, yet we often stumble over this very simplicity. For this reason, Paul's prayers are intensely focused on keeping believers established in all that Jesus has done and will do for us. To give us deeper understanding of Paul's prayers when we study them, let us first review what it looks like for followers of Jesus to abide, obey, love, and trust God in the simplicity of devotion to Christ.

SIMPLE ABIDING

As we learned in the last Chapter, Jesus fulfilled the Old Covenant and the Law of God in perfect righteousness and obedience. He said that the Law and the Prophets could be summarized in two commandments, which are to love the Lord your God with all your heart, soul, mind, and might, and to love your neighbor as yourself. (see Matthew 22:37-39; Deuteronomy 6:5; Leviticus 19:18) Because He fulfilled these on our behalf, we no longer have to strive to measure up to God's standard in order to receive His love and be blessed by Him. Through our faith in

Jesus, our sins and failures are not counted against us and we can be free from guilt, shame, and fear because God sees us as having a perfect record no matter what we do. (see Romans 8:1-2)

This said, Jesus gave a new command to us who follow Him, "Love one another as I have loved you." (see John 13:34, 15:12-17) With this, He entirely changed the configuration and flow of love and blessing. Under the old system, adherents exhaust themselves attempting to love God with all their heart and then, as if there is anything left after using all of their heart, to love others as themselves. But, in the new way of Christ, we as believers receive love unconditionally, freely, and bountifully from God and then are full and able to freely give out what we have received from Him.

This is part of what I call God's "you first" policy. We cannot give out what we have not received for ourselves. If a "you first" policy seems selfish and un-Christian to you, then I urge you to consider how it was so important to the Father that Jesus was assured of His love for Him that before Jesus began His ministry, and at certain other significant moments, God spoke from Heaven in an audible voice in order for His Son (and everyone else around) to unquestionably know of His love and approval. (see Matthew 3:17, 17:5; Mark 11:1; Luke 3:22, 9:35) In the same way, because of what Jesus did for us, we can be assured of God's love for us before we have done anything to deserve it. (see Ephesians 2:8-9) But, in order for us to love others as Jesus loves us, we have to let Him love us first.

In fact, Jesus tells His followers to abide in His love. To *abide* means *to remain, not depart from, continue, endure in, to be held and kept,* and *to wait.*

> *John 15:1-9 ESV - "I am the true vine, and my Father is the vinedresser. Every branch in me that does not bear fruit he takes away, and every branch that does bear fruit he prunes, that it may bear more fruit. Already you are clean because of the word that I have spoken to you. Abide in me, and I in you. As the branch cannot bear fruit by itself, unless it abides in the vine, neither can you, unless you abide in me. I am the vine; you are the branches.*

24

Whoever abides in me and I in him, he it is that bears much fruit, for apart from me you can do nothing. If anyone does not abide in me he is thrown away like a branch and withers; and the branches are gathered, thrown into the fire, and burned. If you abide in me, and my words abide in you, ask whatever you wish, and it will be done for you. By this my Father is glorified, that you bear much fruit and so prove to be my disciples. As the Father has loved me, so have I loved you. Abide in my love.

Practically speaking, to *abide* means to believe that all Jesus died to give us is ours to freely receive and to *not depart* from believing it. It means to *continue* to allow God to have His way in our life and grow deeper in our understanding and application of it in our lives. It means leaving the old behind and *enduring* as a new creation, being led by the Holy Spirit within us. It means to *wait* for God's guidance and to trust that He is working all things out for our good no matter what we do or do not do and no matter what we encounter in life. (see Romans 8:1, 14, 28) It means *remaining* in heavenly places and keeping our thoughts on things above and not on our circumstances. (see Philippians 4:8; Colossians 3:1-2) Most significantly, it means *being held and kept* in His presence so that we can receive the fullness of all that He has for us.

Abiding can be hard work. This said, in truth, it is the only work that God requires of us.

John 6:29 NLT - Jesus told them, "This is the only work God wants from you: Believe in the one he has sent."

For this reason, we need to do whatever is necessary to rearrange our lives and our priorities in order to do it. This may mean spending time in God's presence and keeping Him first in our lives even if this causes other priorities to receive less of our attention and energy. It may mean reading and meditating on His Word rather than watching television or reading other books. It means doing anything that helps us to know God's love and hear His voice, even at the expense of everything else in our lives.

In every other form of work in this world, there is sweat and toil. But in this work of abiding and believing, there is eternal rest and life and peace. (see Hebrews 4:11) People perish because they do not abide and, therefore, do not know God's love and all that He wants to do for us. (see Hosea 4:6; Colossians 2:2) But as we abide, we are filled with a deeper and more intimate knowledge of God and His love for us. Every hindrance is removed, wounds are healed, wrong thinking is replaced with truth, all fear is expelled, and we stop striving for acceptance from anyone other than the One who already accepts us and who is the only One that really matters. This makes us free to love and frees us up to obey God's voice and truly fulfill His purposes.

SIMPLE OBEDIENCE

The Christian life is not a democracy. It is a monarchy—we have a King. Fortunately, our King is our friend and speaks to us clearly through His Spirit so that we can represent Him well as His ambassadors. (see John 15:15; 2 Corinthians 5:20) As God's beloved children and Jesus' sheep, we are each individually able to hear God's voice. (see John 10:4, 14, 27) This means that we have no need for any other person to speak to God for us or to us for God, and we no longer have to guess what God's will is for us. We can stop presuming and hypothetically imitating Jesus or other people whom we believe to be godly because we can simply listen to God for ourselves and be led by the Holy Spirit directly.

> *1 John 2:27 NLT - But you have received the Holy Spirit, and he lives within you, so you don't need anyone to teach you what is true. For the Spirit teaches you everything you need to know, and what he teaches is true--it is not a lie. So just as he has taught you, remain in fellowship with Christ.*

> *John 10:14, 27 - "I am the good shepherd; I know my sheep and my sheep know me-- ... My sheep listen to my voice; I know them, and they follow me.*

> *Hebrews 3:7-8 - So, as the Holy Spirit says: "Today, if you hear his voice, do not harden your hearts as you did in the rebellion, during the time of testing in the wilderness. (see also Hebrews 4:7-11)*

Sometimes, our approach to obedience can become overly passive in the name of "God's sovereignty" thinking that God has predetermined His will and it is both totally inescapable and unaffected by the choices of man. Other times, we can think that doing God's will lies entirely on our ability to obey Him perfectly or the rest of eternity could be altered by our decisions. Another methodology is to make plans according to what we believe to be the good things that God desires for us to be doing and then ask God to bless what we do. However, none of these reflect the relationship of Father and child cooperating to bring about God's will on the earth. To put it plainly, God does have His will, and He gives us free will to cooperate with Him or not. God's will was Eden. Adam's free will messed it up. (see Genesis 3) Jesus, on the other hand, surrendered His free will in order to do only what the Father wanted. On a daily basis and even a moment-by-moment basis, Jesus said and did only what He heard and saw His Father doing by living in obedience to the Holy Spirit. (see John 4:34, 5:19, 6:38, 12:49)

Obedience is simple. All we have to do is listen to God and do what He says. In fact, this is our New Covenant form of worship. Under the old system, the life of an animal was offered to God as a sacrifice of worship. But Jesus, leading the way for us to follow, offered His own life through obedience to His Father, even unto death. Even though He could have used His *Son of God* status and power for His own benefit, He chose to submit Himself entirely to doing His Father's will by dying on the cross. We follow a crucified King.

> *Philippians 2:5-8 - In your relationships with one another, have the same mindset as Christ Jesus: Who, being in very nature God, did not consider equality with God something to be used to his own advantage; rather, he made himself nothing by taking the very nature of a servant, being made in human likeness. And being found in appearance as a man, he humbled himself by becoming obedient to death-- even death on a cross!*

> *Romans 12:1 - Therefore, I urge you, brothers and sisters, in view of God's mercy, to offer your bodies as a living sacrifice, holy and pleasing to God--this is your true and proper worship.*

Jesus does not ask us to do anything for Him that He has not already done Himself. This is another part of God's "you first" policy. When situations and people tempt us into old behavior patterns and we want to confront them in their sin and selfishness, desiring secretly in our hearts to crucify them, God says to us, "you first." God never leads us in hypocrisy. Before we can rebuke anyone for their faults, we must consider our own flesh, selfish ambitions, and preferences to be as good as a dead sacrifice on the altar of God so that we can live to obey His voice, do His will, and not be offended by the flesh of others in order to truly love them. We learn obedience by submitting to God's will and ways of doing things even at the expense of our desires, pride, plans, timing, reputation, and way of doing things. (see Hebrews 5:8, 12:3-11; James 1:4; Romans 5:3-5) In everything that we encounter, the Holy Spirit reveals God's path for us, shows us God's standard of purity, and strengthens us to do things God's way so that like, Jesus, we live our lives in a way that says to God, "Not my will but Yours be done." (see Luke 22:42)

> *Romans 8:5-6, 12-14 - Those who live according to the flesh have their minds set on what the flesh desires; but those who live in accordance with the Spirit have their minds set on what the Spirit desires. The mind governed by the flesh is death, but the mind governed by the Spirit is life and peace. ... Therefore, brothers and sisters, we have an obligation--but it is not to the flesh, to live according to it. For if you live according to the flesh, you will die; but if by the Spirit you put to death the misdeeds of the body, you will live. For those who are led by the Spirit of God are the children of God.*

> *Galatians 5:16-17, 24-25 - So I say, walk by the Spirit, and you will not gratify the desires of the flesh. For the flesh desires what is contrary to the Spirit, and the Spirit what is contrary to the flesh. They are in conflict with each other, so that you are not to do whatever you want. ... Those who belong to Christ Jesus have crucified the flesh with its passions and desires. Since we live by the Spirit, let us keep in step with the Spirit.*

> *John 6:63 - The Spirit gives life; the flesh counts for nothing. The words I have spoken to you--they are full of the Spirit and life.*

> *Matthew 26:41 - "Watch and pray so that you will not fall into*

temptation. The spirit is willing, but the flesh is weak."

As we walk in obedience to the promptings of the Holy Spirit, we quickly discover that God's ways of doing things are much different from our natural inclinations, common sensibilities, short-term and long-term objectives, and earthly perspectives. God knows the end from the beginning and often uses supernatural or miraculous methods of executing His plans because His ways are a lot higher than ours and have a holy and eternal objective. (see Isaiah 55:8-11) For this reason, He often leads us in ways that make absolutely no earthly sense whatsoever in order to demonstrate His love, mercy, and power and so that His name is exalted.

> *1 Corinthians 1:27-29 - But God chose the foolish things of the world to shame the wise; God chose the weak things of the world to shame the strong. God chose the lowly things of this world and the despised things--and the things that are not--to nullify the things that are, so that no one may boast before him.*

God doesn't really need our help. He wants our cooperation as His children as He fulfills His eternal plans in all the earth. Sometimes, it seems that He tells us everything because we are His friends and other times, it seems that we are on a need-to-know basis because if He told us everything our minds would explode. This said, when we trust that He loves us and is working for our good and the good of others, we are free to obey even when we don't know exactly what He is doing. In fact, we stop trusting in ourselves and our own ways and truly begin to know to the depths of our being that God is real and He is good to us. Through this, our mind, will, and emotions are changed to be like Jesus as we keep our attention on Him and press into deeper levels of knowing and doing God's will for our lives.

> *Romans 12:2 - Do not conform to the pattern of this world, but be transformed by the renewing of your mind. Then you will be able to test and approve what God's will is--his good, pleasing and perfect will. (see also James 3:15-17; Galatians 5:19-23)*

> *Philippians 2:13 - for it is God who works in you to will and to act in order to fulfill his good purpose.*

29

2 Corinthians 3:18 - And we all, who with unveiled faces contemplate the Lord's glory, are being transformed into his image with ever-increasing glory, which comes from the Lord, who is the Spirit.

Although submission may sound like subjection, obedience to God is the only submission that leads to absolute liberty. When we do what God asks of us, nothing more and nothing less, we can obey and walk away because we are not responsible for the results...God is. When we have followed the promptings of the Holy Spirit, we can have a clear conscience and be confident that we have done what God asked of us, even if we do not see tangible change right away. Moreover, we can trust that God will reward our obedience. This means that we do not have to look for recognition, approval, or anything in return from those whom we serve. Because of all of these things, obedience to God sets us free to truly love.

SIMPLE LOVE

As we set out to love, undoubtedly, unlovable people cross our paths and it seems that they have been placed there for the singular purpose of aggravating us and revealing to the world just how poorly skilled we are at being like Jesus. But, this is exactly the time for us to overlook their offenses and even to bless them. (see Matthew 5:39-48) That aggravating person is dead in Christ's death (just like we are), and their sins have already been judged (just like ours have been). This means that we don't have a right to judge them because God already has. If they are a believer, then they are a new creation in Christ even though they may not be behaving like one. What they need is encouragement to know who they really are as a child of God. If they are not a believer, then they are still someone for whom Christ died, and what they need is to hear how much He loves them.

Loving others is another part of God's "you first" policy. All of us want the love and acceptance of other people, but first we have to pour out the love that we have received from God whether others love us back or not. Again, Jesus is our example and love is His nature to the core—even in all of His thoughts. While He walked on the earth, He was so connected to

His Father's heart that He knew exactly what the Father wanted done in each situation that He encountered. Jesus did not function to serve any of man's whims or even their immediate needs or demands (see John 11:6), but rather He exclusively, single-mindedly, and whole-heartedly served God and entrusted Himself to His Father alone. (see John 2:24-25) Through this kind of love, the eternal needs of all mankind were met, not to mention the innumerable temporal blessings for those along His path. Moreover, while He was at it, He was loving and merciful in all that He did. He was never unkind or rude. He wasn't jealous and He didn't hold a grudge or keep track of how many times His disciples said or did stupid things. This is just the way that He is. Even today, He never demands loyalty or suppresses His followers. He just loves.

Love is simple, but it is not easy. It can be hard to know what love looks like sometimes. The right approach to loving one person could be a disservice to another depending on where they are in life and what God has purposed for them. (see 1 Thessalonians 5:14) Sometimes love is allowing ourselves to be treated like a doormat while, at other times, love is rebuking a bully. Sometimes love rushes in to help, and other times love does not. The only way to truly love the way that Jesus loves is to be led by the Holy Spirit the way that He was. As we do so, we discover that love is not catering to spoiled impulses and preferences, enabling or endorsing error, encouraging fleshly lusts or worldly desires, or serving needs towards false ambitions. Love is not turning people into our discipleship projects, conforming them to our image or the patterns of our culture, or creating false dependencies. Love is pointing people to the Father and extending mercy and grace to them as their imperfections are revealed. Love is sticking to God's plan for our lives even if everyone else abandons, rejects, and betrays us and even if we look like a complete and total failure from the perspective of man, the world, or even the church because we are trusting in what God is doing as we obey His voice. (see Luke 9:23-26; 14:25-33) Love is helping others to stand firm in God's will, plan, and path for their life no matter how hard it gets and leaving them in God's hands when necessary so that their faith is firmly established in Him alone. (see Hebrews 3:13, 10:24; 1 Thessalonians 5:11) Love is never giving up or losing hope that a person we love can be saved and set free from the pain and torments that afflict them so that they can be transformed into all that God has designed them to be.

> *1 Corinthians 13:4-8a - Love is patient, love is kind. It does not envy, it does not boast, it is not proud. It does not dishonor others, it is not self-seeking, it is not easily angered, it keeps no record of wrongs. Love does not delight in evil but rejoices with the truth. It always protects, always trusts, always hopes, always perseveres. Love never fails.*

In the world's kind of love, there is fear and hidden selfishness such as, "Will they love me back?", "What if I lose what I love?", or "What if I get hurt by loving so much?" But in God's kind of love, there is life and Jesus even called it His food. (see 1 John 4:16-17; John 4:24) This kind of love can be selfless because our love does not depend on anything or anyone other than our relationship and our trust in God—our loving Heavenly Father.

SIMPLE TRUST

Let's be honest. If Jesus is not who He says that He is, then we who believe Him are deceived people with martyr complexes and the biggest fools on earth. However, since He is who He says He is, we have to learn to trust Him. Again, as part of God's "you first" policy, we have no business telling anyone else to trust Him if we do not trust Him first for ourselves.

I have found that it is easier to trust God to work in my life and in the lives of others when I understand exactly what God says He is going to do. I certainly don't want to be trusting Him to do something for me that He never said He would do for me. Equally so, I don't want to be trusting Him to do something for someone else that He wants me to go and do on His behalf for them. Also, because God is so much better at everything than I am, I do not want to intervene and do something that He wants to do for me or for anyone else. Fortunately for us, God makes it pretty clear what our part is and what His part is. For example:

> *Matthew 6:33 - But seek first his kingdom and his righteousness, and all these things will be given to you as well.*

Psalm 37:4 - Take delight in the LORD, and he will give you the desires of your heart.

Proverbs 3:5-6 - Trust in the LORD with all your heart and lean not on your own understanding; in all your ways submit to him, and he will make your paths straight.

Sometimes trusting God is as unsophisticated as believing that He is a rewarder of those who seek Him (see Hebrews 11:6) even if we feel like we do not know what we are doing. Other times, it means completely taking our hands off of a situation in order to get out of God's way and allow Him to work it out according to His will. (see John 6:29; Zechariah 4:6) Then again, there are times that God asks us to wholeheartedly jump into doing something completely foreign to us so that we depend entirely on Him as we do it. (see 2 Corinthians 1:9) As a matter of fact, when we start truly relying upon God in deeper levels of trust and obedience, it seems that He leads us straight into situations which appear to be the exact opposite of what He promised us. The journey between spiritual immaturity and spiritual maturity is what I call "a walk with the Lord through the valley of the shadow of death." (see Psalm 23:4) The path of true greatness includes being willing to be nothing so that God can truly be everything. He leads us through obscurity, failure, humiliation, isolation, and various other trials so that we learn to rely upon His faithfulness to bring about what He promised rather than relying on our own strength, abilities, intellect, or skills and so that we fear no evil because we have learned to trust Him.

While we walk with God in deeper and deeper levels of dependence on Him, it can be helpful to know the job descriptions of the Holy Spirit. If the Holy Spirit does not do His job then God is a liar. Since God is not a liar, we can trust Him to do these things, especially when we cannot see with our eyes or in our circumstances that He is at work. For starters, Jesus said this about what the Holy Spirit does:

John 16:8-11 ESV - And when he [the Holy Spirit] comes, he will convict the world concerning sin and righteousness and judgment: concerning sin, because they do not believe in me; concerning righteousness, because I go to the Father, and you will see me no longer; concerning judgment, because the ruler of this world is judged.

The Holy Spirit is the only one who can truly convert those who do not yet believe Jesus. He also makes it known that they are disconnected from God due to sin, that Jesus is God's plumb line and standard of uprightness, character, and goodness, that the world's ways are more in line with the evil one, and that faith in Jesus is the only way to be spared from eternal condemnation. (see Amos 7:7-8; Isaiah 28:16-17; John 3:18-19) Equally so, for those who do believe Jesus, the Holy Spirit is the only one who can expose the areas of unbelief in our lives where we are not fully trusting Jesus for the things that He freely gives us in a way that brings lasting change. He also helps us to know that we share in all the blessings of the righteous through our faith in Jesus and that we have victory over the evil one who has been defeated through Jesus' death and resurrection. All of this means that our salvation and growth to spiritual maturity is the Holy Spirit's job from start to finish. All we have to do is believe God and let Him do His job by not resisting Him as He works and by doing what He says when He speaks.

The chart on the next page details some other things that the Holy Spirit does. (This is not an all-inclusive list.)

ROLES AND FUNCTIONS OF THE HOLY SPIRIT	
Holy Spirit Job Description	Scriptures
Births us as children of God and gives us life	John 3:5-8, 6:63; 2 Corinthians 3:6; Romans 8:2, 11
Regenerates us, purifies us, sanctifies us, gives us the fruit of the spirit and the character of Christ	John 16:8-11; 1 Corinthians 6:11; Romans 15:16; 2 Corinthians 3:18; 1 Peter 1:2; 2 Thessalonians 2:13; Titus 3:5; Galatians 5:22-23
Speaks to us and through us	Acts 2:4, 4:31, 8:29, 10:19, 11:12, 28, 21:4; John 15:26-27, 16:13; Mark 13:11
Teaches us and reveals the deep things and mysteries of God	Luke 12:12; Acts 6:10; John 14:26, 16:13; 1 Corinthians 2:10-14; Ephesians 1:17
Guides us in the way of God	Acts 1:2, 8:29, 10:19, 11:28, 13:4, 16:6-7, 20:22-23; Galatians 5:18; Romans 8:14; John 16:13; Luke 22:26; Mark 1:12
Encourages us, comforts us, helps us in our weaknesses, intercedes for us according to God's will	John 14:26; Acts 9:31; Romans 8:26-27; 1 Corinthians 14:14
Gives us power from God for ministry	Acts 1:8; Luke 4:14, 18-19; Ephesians 3:16; 1 Corinthians 2:4; Romans 15:19
Empowers us with spiritual gifts, and with prophecy, dreams, and visions	Acts 2:4, 17-18; 11:28; Hebrews 2:4; 1 Corinthians 12:4, 7-13, 14:2; Revelation 19:10; 2 Peter 1:21

With the Holy Spirit taking care of all of these things, we can relax and let Him do His job in our lives and in the lives of others. We can stop telling God how to do His job in our lives, and we can stop bossing other people around or manipulating them to get our own way because we trust that God is working it all out for us and for them in His way, in His timing, and for His purposes. He has been God for a very long time and He knows what He is doing! We have been set free from performance based rules and standards so that our trust can be in God alone and so that we can be led by the Holy Spirit as His beloved children.

Romans 8:14-15 - For those who are led by the Spirit of God are the children of God. The Spirit you received does not make you slaves, so that you live in fear again; rather, the Spirit you received brought about your adoption to sonship. And by him we cry, "Abba, Father." (see also Galatians 4:6)

2 Timothy 1:7 NKJV - For God has not given us a spirit of fear, but of power and of love and of a sound mind.

Most importantly, since so many weighty responsibilities have been lifted off of us because they are the Holy Spirit's job, we are free to receive God's love and to love other people just as they are and wherever they may be in life or in their walk with the Lord. Now we can simply and fearlessly cooperate with our loving Heavenly Father and leave the rest in His hands because we trust Him. This said, the only way to build trust in God is to start trusting Him. If He is really God (and He is), then we have nothing to fear.

PAUL'S EXAMPLE

Not everyone is called to martyrdom, but every believer is called to take up their cross, crucify their flesh, and follow Jesus. Not everyone is called to give away everything that they own, but every believer is called to love nothing more than Jesus and to cling to nothing of this world. Not everyone is called to be like the Apostle Paul but every believer is called to be like Jesus, and each one of us has a role and a purpose in God's Kingdom.

This said, the Apostle Paul gave us an example of a person whose life was entirely devoted to Christ.[1] He had been a passionate Pharisee with the best training in the Scriptures that the world had to offer at that time. He had been on a mission to eradicate Christianity from the face of the earth and to kill any Christians who would not deny that Jesus is Lord. But after an encounter with the living Lord Jesus on the road to Damascus, Paul became a believer. Then, following his conversion, he went into the

---

[1] *The story of Paul's conversion and transformation can be found in Acts 9:3-9, 11:25-30, 13:1-3, 22:3-21, 26:1-23; Philippians 3:3-9; Galatians 1:13-2:1; 2 Corinthians 11*

wilderness of Arabia for three years. During this time, the Lord revealed to Paul that all the Scriptures point to Him (see John 5:39) and have been fulfilled through His death and resurrection. Paul's extensive knowledge of the Scriptures was converted from the perspective of a condemning Law-enforcer to the Lord's heart of love, grace, mercy, and faith.

Paul's approach to life was also completely renovated. Following his conversion, Paul was rejected by his old comrades as a traitor, heretic, brainwashed idiot, and runaway. At the same time, the people in the Church did not believe that Paul had really become a follower of Jesus so they were afraid of him and did not accept him either. Paul did not care what they thought or what happened to his career, or to any part of life as he had known it. This was his mindset:

> *Philippians 3:7-9 - But whatever were gains to me I now consider loss for the sake of Christ. What is more, I consider everything a loss because of the surpassing worth of knowing Christ Jesus my Lord, for whose sake I have lost all things. I consider them garbage, that I may gain Christ and be found in him, not having a righteousness of my own that comes from the law, but that which is through faith in Christ--the righteousness that comes from God on the basis of faith.*

After the wilderness in Arabia, Paul spent over ten years in Cilicia and historians are not certain exactly what he was doing while he was there. No doubt, Paul was wholly devoted to the Lord, but it did not seem that God was using Paul too powerfully at all, at least for a season. But, all the while, God was transforming Paul from a religious zealot into the most influential advocate for Christianity that the world has ever known.

Eventually, believers from the church at Antioch came to fetch Paul and bring him back in order to teach the church in the ways of the Lord. Soon enough, the Holy Spirit set Paul apart for ministry and his missionary journeys began. Paul and his teams changed the world through the proclamation of the Gospel, first to the Jew and then to the Gentile, in every territory where the Lord sent him. Paul endured through persecution, riots, beatings, imprisonments, and attacks by false teachers and joyously suffered for the name of Jesus. He was eventually beheaded for our faith, is now with the Lord in glory, and will rule and reign with Jesus for 1,000 years. (see Revelation 20:4-5) The Church as we know it today was largely established through Paul's simple devotion to Christ.

After establishing churches in various cities, Paul received updates about their progress, struggles, successes, failures, and persecution that they were encountering in their area of the world. He wrote letters to encourage and guide them in the ways of God and His grace. His letters included the prayers he prayed night and day for them and the prayers he requested for himself. Paul's prayers do not contain an ounce of hypocrisy but were genuine from the heart of a transformed man who knew the love of God and who had laid down his own life for the name of Jesus. He unquestionably adhered to God's "you first" policy, leading us all in what it means to truly worship God and follow Jesus.

CHAPTER THREE
FOR BELIEVERS
AND THOSE WHO WILL BE

OH, MY DEAR CHILDREN! I FEEL AS IF I'M GOING
THROUGH LABOR PAINS FOR YOU AGAIN, AND
THEY WILL CONTINUE UNTIL CHRIST IS FULLY
DEVELOPED IN YOUR LIVES.
– THE APOSTLE PAUL, GALATIANS 4:19 NLT

The prayers of the Apostle Paul reflect his heart for all believers to grow to spiritual maturity and to walk in the fullness of all that Christ died to give us. He desired for everyone to have a deep and genuine experience of God's faithfulness through knowing Jesus personally for ourselves. When Jesus was on the earth, He gave His disciples only one prayer to pray:

Matthew 6:9-13 - "This, then, is how you should pray: 'Our Father in heaven, hallowed be your name, your kingdom come, your will be done, on earth as it is in heaven. Give us today our daily bread. And forgive us our debts, as we also have forgiven our debtors. And lead us not into temptation, but deliver us from the evil one.'"

Paul's prayers reflect this profound minimalism and cleanness but offer us more clarifications than the Lord's prayer affords because Paul was praying for specific groups of disciples who were dealing with particular trials and attacks against the Christian faith. This said, even though they were written to actual believers during a certain period of time to encourage them in their various travails, they hold profound relevance for us today as we follow Jesus and pursue all that He has for us.

GROW IN THE KNOWLEDGE OF GOD (EPHESIANS 1:15-23)

Ephesus was a city enamored with spiritual power in all of its various forms. The Ephesian church started with about twelve men, but when the Apostle Paul arrived and proclaimed the Gospel many people repented from their various forms of spirituality and placed their trust in Jesus. For the next two and a half years, Paul stayed in Ephesus, and God confirmed his ministry with powerful miracles. Soon enough, some exorcists traveling through Ephesus bootlegged the name of Jesus without becoming believers themselves, but it did not work out too well for them because the demons that they were attempting to exorcise beat them up. When word of this spread, even more people placed their faith in Jesus and set a colossal bonfire of repentance in the center of the city to burn all of their spirituality propaganda which was not rooted in Christ. Of course, this was not good for those who made their living making idols. So, the idol makers started a riot against Paul and the Ephesian believers. After the riot dispersed, Paul departed on his way to Macedonia, but the intense persecution and pressure to return to false spirituality continued in Ephesus. (For more on Paul's time in Ephesus, see Acts 19) Later, when Paul prayed for the elders of the church at Ephesus, he did so with heartfelt encouragement and tearful warnings about keeping the believers true to the purity of the Gospel and watching out for false teachers. (see Acts 20:13-38) Several years after that, while imprisoned for the name of Jesus, Paul wrote his letter to the believers of the Ephesian church to remind them of the great love of God for those who believe His Son and of the Kingdom power that He has made available to His people.

This was Paul's prayer:

> Ephesians 1:15-23 - For this reason, ever since I heard about your faith in the Lord Jesus and your love for all God's people, I have not stopped giving thanks for you, remembering you in my prayers. I keep asking that the God of our Lord Jesus Christ, the glorious Father, may give you the Spirit of wisdom and revelation, so that you may know him better. I pray that the eyes of your heart may be enlightened in order that you may know the hope to which he has called you, the riches of his glorious inheritance in his holy people, and his incomparably great power

for us who believe. That power is the same as the mighty strength he exerted when he raised Christ from the dead and seated him at his right hand in the heavenly realms, far above all rule and authority, power and dominion, and every name that is invoked, not only in the present age but also in the one to come. And God placed all things under his feet and appointed him to be head over everything for the church, which is his body, the fullness of him who fills everything in every way.

In this prayer, Paul essentially prayed only two things for believers. First, that God would give an increased measure of the Holy Spirit and second, that our hearts would be opened to receive it. He knew that the Holy Spirit is the only one who could give true and pure wisdom and revelation from God. This said, God gives wisdom to anyone who asks for it but when He does so, we must believe that God has shown us His way and receive His counsel for our lives. This is more challenging than it may sound, but this is only because God's wisdom often sounds like foolishness to our common sensibilities and the ways of this world.

James 1:5-6 - If any of you lacks wisdom, you should ask God, who gives generously to all without finding fault, and it will be given to you. But when you ask, you must believe and not doubt, because the one who doubts is like a wave of the sea, blown and tossed by the wind.

1 Corinthians 2:12-16 - What we have received is not the spirit of the world, but the Spirit who is from God, so that we may understand what God has freely given us. This is what we speak, not in words taught us by human wisdom but in words taught by the Spirit, explaining spiritual realities with Spirit-taught words. The person without the Spirit does not accept the things that come from the Spirit of God but considers them foolishness, and cannot understand them because they are discerned only through the Spirit. The person with the Spirit makes judgments about all things, but such a person is not subject to merely human judgments, for, "Who has known the mind of the Lord so as to instruct him?" But we have the mind of Christ.

41

James 3:17 - But the wisdom that comes from heaven is first of all pure; then peace-loving, considerate, submissive, full of mercy and good fruit, impartial and sincere.

1 Corinthians 1:25 - For the foolishness of God is wiser than human wisdom, and the weakness of God is stronger than human strength.

Along the same lines, the Holy Spirit is the only one who can give revelation knowledge that penetrates and governs our lives in the ways of God. The word *revelation* is *apokalypsis,* and this is the origin of our word in English for *apocalypse.* When God gives revelation knowledge and we open our hearts to receive it, it is like a mini apocalypse in our hearts and minds. Like a lightning bolt in our souls, all of a sudden, we comprehend something that we have not understood before and we also have an unexplainable power to apply this new knowledge to our lives. We have no ability to force the things that we know about God and His love in our minds to penetrate into our hearts and in fact, it does not work that way. Rather, revelation comes from the new heart and new spirit that God has put within us and as we listen and cooperate, the Holy Spirit dispatches pure and loving guidance from God. If we receive and believe what God reveals to us, then His counsel infuses our way of thinking and is coupled with emotional strength and willpower to put it into practice.

Paul prayed these things so that believers would grow in our knowledge of God. The word for *knowledge* used here means *precise and correct knowledge of God's divine nature,* and even *experiential knowledge of God.* We need to know that God is love, God is good, God is all-powerful, all-knowing, all-seeing, unchanging, and on our side because of Jesus. (see 1 John 4:8; Romans 8:31) This said, knowing about God is simply not enough to strengthen us to stand in faith when trials and temptations come. We need to know God for ourselves through our own experience of His faithfulness. The evil one is the most subtle of all creatures at distracting us from accurately understanding the ways of God and at creating counterfeit opportunities in an attempt to cause us to stumble. (see Genesis 3:1) Practically speaking, I have heard it said that counterfeit currency experts do not spend their time studying fake money. Instead, they spend all of their time inspecting and becoming intimately familiar with the real thing. Then, when a phony shows up, they can identify it instantly because they know the genuine article so well. In the same way, when we truly know God, including His nature and His ways, we will not be easily swayed away from placing our trust in Him alone.

Paul also desired for believers to know the hope that we have been called to in Christ. We have been born again to a living hope and to an eternal inheritance of heaven and even heaven on earth. (1 Peter 1:3-4; Ephesians 1:10-11) The Biblical word for *hope* is not the same as our common word for hope. Our word for hope indicates an uncertain optimism, like when we really want something to happen but we are not really sure if it will happen or not. In contrast, the Biblical word means *confident expectation of a future event,* and even more so, *confident expectation of good.* Before we were saved, we had no eternal hope at all. But at the moment we believed Jesus, we were marked with the Holy Spirit as a deposit to guarantee what is coming to us for all eternity. (see Ephesians 1:13) This means that we can confidently expect that God will fulfill all of His promises of good towards us, both in this age and in the age to come. Moreover, our hope is not a stagnant hope of something that is far away in the future, but rather our confident expectation of heaven in the future is alive and active and accessible to us now through our faith. We have authority in the name of Jesus to receive and to dispense heaven's salvation, deliverance, healing, sustenance, and to bring the Kingdom of God to earth right now as it is in heaven without disrupting our eternal inheritance. In fact, the way that we live our lives now is always a direct reflection of our perspective of eternity and our understanding of our eternal hope. If we are truly the only people on earth who have a legitimate eternal hope, which we are, and we know that at the end of the age we will inherit and rule the whole world, which we will, then we can stop contending against one another over temporal things because we trust that God will make all things right for us in the end. If only the Church would know this hope!

Paul's prayer indicates his yearning for believers to know how precious we are to God as His people because we are His eternal inheritance. Since the beginning of mankind, God desired a people for Himself who will worship Him, glorify His name in the earth, and to whom He can pour out His love and abundance as the object of His affection. Unfortunately, history shows that the people that God has chosen to be His own have not handled it very well. Adam messed up his special status with God by eating from the wrong tree. Later, the people of Israel, the only people on the earth with a relationship with the one true God, continually rebelled against God's ways and His prophets until they ultimately rejected and killed Jesus, their own Messiah. Oy vey. But now, through our faith in Jesus, we are God's children and His prized possession. What is even better is that, because our sins are forgiven by the blood of Jesus, our Adam-like tendency toward wrong choices and our Israelite-ish bent towards being stubborn and stiff-necked against Him cannot deprecate us in God's sight. This means that God finally has a people that He can love and bless without being hindered by our faults and failures! God has chosen us to be the object of His affection and blessing, and He will move mountains for us because He loves us with all of His heart. (see Jeremiah 32:41) If only we knew how precious we are to Him!

Paul finished his prayer with a proclamation and reminder to believers of our inclusion in Christ's ascension to the throne room of heaven and that Jesus is the highest spiritual authority in all creation. No other form of spirituality can compete or compare with the power of God through Jesus Christ. The Gospel *is* the power of the one true God who created heaven and earth. Through the Gospel, this power has been made available to us for salvation, deliverance, healing, and sustenance. Or, in other words, the Gospel is everything we will ever need for every trial that we will face between now and when we leave this world to be with the Lord. (see Romans 1:16-17) The same power that raised Jesus from the dead now dwells within us who believe that He is Lord and no one in the world, except the true Church, has access to it. In fact, it is this power which gives us the life of God in our mortal bodies to strengthen us to say, "No" to sin, to false spirituality, to worldliness, to the evil one, and to all the forces at work in this world that seek to gain dominance in our lives. Indeed, the role of the Church on the earth is to demonstrate and to make known the superiority of Christ by not bowing down to any other power and by having no dependencies in our lives on anything other than Jesus because Jesus is truly all that we need. (see Ephesians 3:10) It is our fearless trust in God's love for us that silences competing voices in this world and demonstrates Christ's preeminence to all the spiritual powers of darkness and to unbelievers. (see Philippians 1:28) For this reason, our aim should be (as was Paul's) to know nothing except Jesus Christ who was crucified and to receive all of God's benefits for ourselves in order to reveal the power and goodness of God towards those of us who place our trust in Jesus. (see 1 Corinthians 2:2; Philippians 3:12)

Notably, Paul did not pray against the evil one, did not lower himself or us to the enemy's playing field, and did not entangle himself in arguments against the schemes of men or other forms of spirituality. Instead, his prayer emphasized, in every possible way, that Jesus triumphed over sin, death, the devil, and all the forces of evil in this world. He wanted us to know that *"It is finished!"* We do not fight against the powers of this world or even against flesh and blood with weapons of man or even with plausible arguments. On the contrary, when we reject the arguments and false promises of this world and show by our faith in the Lord alone that we do not require all the things the world says we so desperately need, we prove the world and all of its gods to be wrong. (see 2 Corinthians 10:4-5) As followers of Christ, our lives are now centered on the spiritual realities of heaven and not earthly things, circumstances, or even people. Because of this, we can refrain from endless debates and arguments because the Kingdom of God is not in talk but in revealing heaven's power through Jesus. (see 1 Corinthians 2:2, 4:20) Our work is to know and believe what Christ has done for us, and our only protective armor is to not allow ourselves to be diverted from it. (see Ephesians 6:10-17) May His name be praised forever!

RECEIVE GOD'S LOVE (EPHESIANS 3:14-21)

As Paul continued his prayers for the believers in Ephesus, his letter emphasized what God accomplished through the resurrection of Christ. God created a whole new species in the earth to be His New Covenant people and this makes us who believe Jesus different from His Old Covenant people and also from everyone else in the world who does not yet believe Jesus. Before we trusted Jesus, we were completely estranged from God. If we were Jewish at birth, we had a covenant with God but it was this very covenant which condemned us through our own inability to measure up to God's standard. If we were Gentile (non-Jewish) at birth, we had no connection to the one true God at all and no hope of getting through to Him because of our sinful state which stems all the way back to our first ancestor Adam. This means that, Jew or Gentile, we were all condemned to eternal darkness and separation from God. But now, through our faith in Christ, we have been adopted as God's children. This is the love of God for us! The Creator of the Universe is our Dad and has given us special privileges and access to His unmerited love and blessings!

This was Paul's prayer:

> Ephesians 3:14-21 - For this reason I kneel before the Father, from whom every family in heaven and on earth derives its name. I pray that out of his glorious riches he may strengthen you with power through his Spirit in your inner being, so that Christ may dwell in your hearts through faith. And I pray that you, being rooted and established in love, may have power, together with all the Lord's holy people, to grasp how wide and long and high and deep is the love of Christ, and to know this love that surpasses knowledge--that you may be filled to the measure of all the fullness of God. Now to him who is able to do immeasurably more than all we ask or imagine, according to his power that is at work within us, to him be glory in the church and in Christ Jesus throughout all generations, for ever and ever! Amen.

Again, Paul prayed for two things. First, that God would give believers strength and power in our inmost beings and second, for believers to have power to grasp and to know God's love for us. Paul emphasized that God is able to give the Holy Spirit without measure out of His absolutely limitless resources towards those who believe. He is a good Father and gives good gifts to His children, particularly the Holy Spirit when we ask Him. (see Luke 11:11-13) God's love is abounding towards us and available for us if we will simply believe Him and receive it.

Paul stated that he prayed these things so that Christ could dwell in our hearts by faith. It is the Holy Spirit in our hearts who cries out to God as our Father, and even our Daddy. (see Romans 8:15; Galatians 4:6) Everyone else in the world that cries out to God does so with no assurance of being heard; God can seem distant, cold, harsh, angry, punitive, and unfair. But to us who believe Jesus, the Holy Spirit gives us the heart of a son or daughter of God so that we can draw near to Him, be assured that He hears us and that He is working everything out for our good because He loves us. The only unfairness of God for those of us who believe is that when we had done nothing to deserve it, Christ died in our place so that we could share in His Sonship as God's children. The more we believe in His goodness and love for us and allow Him to work in our hearts, the more of His goodness and love we receive!

Paul's prayer also expressed his heart for all believers to "be filled to the full measure of all the fullness of God" or, in other words, to become spiritually mature. Spiritual maturity is to be like Christ in our nature and to do the things He did the way that He did them. Unlike worldly maturity which focuses on self-sufficiency and independence, spiritual maturity is aimed at child-likeness and absolute dependence on God as our loving heavenly Father. When our trust and dependence are completely and totally in God alone, we become immovably secure in all that we do no matter what kind of resistance or animosity we encounter. When we know that we are loved by God, we stop needing the approval of other people and we stop chasing after fancy teachings which boast about their special access to God's Kingdom because we know that the Kingdom of God is already within us. (see Ephesians 4:13-14; Luke 17:20-23) We grow to maturity by abiding in His love for us and following His guidance for our lives like children who are along for a ride with our Daddy.

Paul closed this prayer by exalting the name of Jesus and the power of God which is at work in the hearts of those who believe. When we allow God to work in our lives and in our hearts, He does something that is exceedingly and abundantly beyond all that we could ever ask or imagine. What He does for us will not be according to the pattern of this world but will conform us to the likeness of His Son because we are His sons and daughters. May we all know God's love for us as our Heavenly Father, so that we are able to love the way that Jesus loves and bring God glory as His children!

ABOUND IN LOVE (PHILIPPIANS 1:9-11)

Paul was beckoned to Macedonia and Philippi by a vision of a man begging to hear the Gospel. Paul proclaimed the Gospel at Philippi and, soon after that, the church was started. One day, Paul commanded a spirit of divination out of a slave girl who was fortune-telling to make money for her owners. This dismantled their profiteering, so they mobbed Paul, beat him, and had him thrown in prison. As Paul and his traveling partner sang songs of praise in their prison cell, a great earthquake broke their shackles off and the awestruck and terrified jailer placed his faith in Jesus. After this, the city officials begged Paul to leave Philippi forever. (For more on Paul's time in Philippi, see Acts 16:6-40) The believers at Philippi gave themselves wholeheartedly to the Lord and continued to do so even after Paul left the city. They extended God's grace to others through extravagant giving in spite of their own poverty and the riotous persecution against them in Philippi. When no one else supported Paul or supplied him with resources for proclaiming the Gospel in various cities, the Philippians gave abundantly so that others could come to know Jesus. (see Philippians 4:15-16) When an offering was taken for the Jewish followers of Jesus in Judea who were struggling in the face of famine, the Philippians begged for the privilege of supplying them materially as an expression of their gratitude for all they had received from them spiritually. (see 2 Corinthians 8:1-5) Paul was overjoyed with the Philippians because their selflessness demonstrated that they truly understood the goodness and love of God for them in Christ. However, at the same time, there were false teachers traveling around who were peddling the name of Jesus for profit and Paul desired for the exceedingly gracious Philippians to be protected from these predators. Paul wrote this letter to the Philippians from prison as a thank you note and an encouragement for all the good that they were doing for the Lord and His people. He also wanted to reassure them that even the worst of trials works out for the glory of God.

This was Paul's prayer:

Philippians 1:9-11 - And this is my prayer: that your love may abound more and more in knowledge and depth of insight, so that you may be able to discern what is best and may be pure and blameless for the day of Christ, filled with the fruit of righteousness that comes through Jesus Christ--to the glory and praise of God.

In this prayer, Paul prayed for believer's love to abound more and more. This *agape* love is what Paul desired for all of us to have and to live out in our lives with the Lord as an expression of His love. For some, it could mean laying down our lives in true martyrdom for Christ while for others it could mean simply giving of our resources and abilities. While there is much to be said for generosity proving the sincerity of our love (see 2 Corinthians 8:8; 1 John 3:15-17; James 2:14-16), money and material giving is not at the heart of what God desires from us. We could give away everything that we have and even sacrificially give of ourselves in the name of Jesus, but if we do so without genuine love in our hearts then it's all a worthless sham. (see 1 Corinthians 13:1-3) God is totally unimpressed with giving that does not flow from a sincere heart, and God is not interested in offerings which are given from a motive of working the system to be blessed in return. What God desires in our heart is genuine mercy, selfless kindness, and joyful giving to others even when they do not deserve it. (see Matthew 9:13, 12:7) When we do this, He sees to it that all of our needs are met and that we are blessed in every imaginable way so that we can love all the more. (see Philippians 4:19; 2 Corinthians 9:11)

Paul desired for our love to be intermingled with knowledge and depth of insight. Again, this *knowledge* is *true and accurate understanding of God,* but in this prayer it is coupled with insight into the practicalities of life. While we are all called to give of ourselves in selflessness, only the Holy Spirit is able to show us what this looks like in our own lives according to God's purpose for us. What is right is not always obvious by what the eye can see but, fortunately, God knows everything and He is nobody's fool. As we follow the promptings of the Holy Spirit and grow to spiritual maturity, we are trained to discern good from evil, right from wrong, and what is vital from what is trivial. (see Hebrews 5:14) Through this, we know how to love, when to give or not give according to God's will in each situation with each person that we encounter. Sometimes, it is loving to give it all, and other times it is God's will for us to give nothing. God knows what He is doing and what He wants us to do. We owe nothing to anyone except to love them, and we do this best when we simply obey the promptings of God.

Paul also articulated that this would keep believers pure and blameless. It is not through our good works or even through our love that we are made holy, blameless, or righteous because God did that for us through Christ's blood, death, and resurrection. (see Hebrews 10:10) However, we have been made holy, blameless, and righteous so that we can be holy, blameless, and righteous in our actions towards others and in our love for them. (see Romans 6:18) It is for this very reason that Christ redeemed us. We have been set free from following rules and regulations so that we can follow the Holy Spirit. By doing so, God shows us how to do the right thing at the right time in the right way and with and for the right people. Walking in this kind of purity keeps our hearts free from evil motives and selfish intentions because we are simply serving God. When we obey God and do whatever we do for Him alone, we do not have to second-guess ourselves, fear punishment for missed opportunities, or regret when others do not receive us well. We can have a totally clear conscience before God and man. What a relief!

Paul's heart was also for us to be filled with the fruit of righteousness. The word for *righteous* in Hebrew can mean both *uprightness* and *justice*. God's justice is totally without fault and, straightforwardly, all who do evil deserve His wrath. However, Jesus introduced an upside-down version of justice where we who do wrong do not get what we deserve because the only One who was truly upright took all of our warranted punishment. (see 2 Corinthians 5:21) This kind of backwards justice is available to everyone who will place his or her faith in Jesus. This said, as we receive this beautiful gift for ourselves, it is God's intention for us to become agents of this same kind of upside-down justice. The *fruit of righteousness* is to be like the Righteous One by turning the other cheek, going the extra mile, blessing and praying for our enemies, and taking up our cross so that the people we encounter can have an experience, not of

God's judgment or wrath, but of His mercy. (see Matthew 5:38-48; Luke 9:23)

Paul's desire was for believers to live our lives in a way that our words and actions declare God's praises for all to hear and to see. Our love shows that we understand what God has done for us. Our discernment without judgmentalism reveals our maturity. May we all continue to grow in these things until Christ returns to take us home.

GROW IN HOLINESS (2 THESSALONIANS 1:11-12)

Paul proclaimed the Gospel in Thessalonica and then had to leave town due to an accusation against him for treason because he was preaching about King Jesus, who was regarded by locals as competition to Caesar. (For more on Paul's time in Thessalonica, see Acts 17:1-9) After Paul left, the persecution against the Thessalonian believers continued to be intense, and Paul feared that they would abandon the faith and return to their old way of life because he had not had much time to train them in God's grace or to teach them from the Scriptures. He sent messengers to report back to him about their progress, only to learn that the Thessalonian believers stood strong in their faith. Needless to say, Paul was elated with relief and love for these budding new creations in Christ. The believers had banded together with one another and it seemed that the hostility against them only served to make them experts at caring for each other. However, because they were mostly Gentile with no foundational knowledge in the Scriptures, they had very little knowledge of God's ways or standards of purity and morality. Without any religious imposition or command, Paul exhorted the Thessalonian believers to live their lives in a way that is pleasing to God and reflected His holiness, particularly in the area of sexual purity. (see 1 Thessalonians 4:3) He knew that if they were going to stand in the faith and persevere through trials, temptations, and tribulations, then they would need to continue to grow and mature in the Lord and His likeness.

This was Paul's prayer:

2 Thessalonians 1:11-12 - With this in mind, we constantly pray for you, that our God may make you worthy of his calling, and that by his power he may bring to fruition your every desire for goodness and your every deed prompted by faith. We pray this so that the name of our Lord Jesus may be glorified in you, and you in him, according to the grace of our God and the Lord Jesus Christ.

Paul prayed that God would make believers worthy of His calling, and he revealed what is at the core of this worthiness from God's point of view.

2 Thessalonians 1:4-5 - Therefore, among God's churches we boast about your perseverance and faith in all the persecutions and trials you are enduring. All this is evidence that God's judgment is right, and as a result you will be counted worthy of the kingdom of God, for which you are suffering.

Faith alone is what causes us to be counted as worthy of the Kingdom of God. The only thing that matters to God is that we trust Him by believing Jesus, no matter what comes against us. As our example, Jesus endured mocking, rejection, a false trial, beating, and crucifixion because He believed that God would resurrect Him on the third day. For this, Jesus is worthy of all glory, honor, and praise, and He is now seated in the place of honor at God's right hand for all eternity. (see Revelation 5:9) Similarly, we as believers are counted worthy of His Kingdom for our faith, which is proven particularly when we suffer joyously and continue praising God in spite of difficult circumstances. (see 1 Peter 1:7)

This said, like Jesus who is also worthy because He is the sinless and spotless Lamb of God, or like athletes in a marathon, we will only receive an eternal prize if we play according to the rules. (see 2 Timothy 2:5) This means living our lives in a way that is a reflection of God's ways of doing things. God has made us holy so that we can be holy. (see 1 Peter 1:16) To be *holy* means to be *set apart* or *consecrated to God for His purposes* and, in this, to be *distinguished from what is common.* After the Holy Spirit comes into our hearts when we first believe Jesus, He begins His work of regenerating us to make us like Christ or, in a word, to make us godly. The same Spirit that governed Jesus' life and strengthened Him to do God's will when He was on the earth is now inside us to guide us and empower us to fulfill God's purposes in His ways. The Holy Spirit within us is the only power by which we will have the ability to stand in our faith against the schemes of the enemy, the lures of this world, and the lusts of our flesh that cause us to stumble into sin or fail to grow to spiritual maturity. We have been made holy by Jesus' sacrifice so that we can be made holy in all of our ways by the work of His Spirit within us.

When God's standards of holy living for His New Covenant people were in question in the early Church, the first apostles gathered together at the Jerusalem Council to seek the Lord and determine the appropriate requirements for followers of Jesus. (see Acts 15:1-31) In Christ, because we have been fully liberated from the Law of God, we are no longer required to obey it in order to have right standing with Him. However, the Law is good and explicitly details God's standard of purity in the event that there is any confusion about what is pleasing to Him. (see 1 Timothy 1:9-11; Romans 7:12) Therefore, in order to reveal God's holiness to those who do not yet believe that Jesus is Lord, the apostles agreed that it was important for followers of Jesus to abstain from eating food offered to idols, from eating blood, and from sexual immorality. (For God's definition of sexual immorality, see Leviticus, Chapter 18.) These things were strictly forbidden in the Law of Moses, and any Jew who knows this would find it difficult to accept the Gospel message from someone doing these things while claiming to follow the Jewish Messiah and worship the God of Israel. Living by the New Covenant standard of faith does not contradict the Old Covenant standard but rather gives us supernatural power to do what is pleasing to God. (see Romans 3:31) Doing things God's way is a demonstration that followers of Jesus are truly set apart from the common way of doing things. Proclaiming the Gospel with our mouths is easy, but it is how we conduct our lives as God's holy people that tells the watching world about the God we serve.

Paul also prayed for God to give believers power to accomplish all the good things our faith prompts us to do. Paul's aim was always that believers would trust God enough to love others selflessly. (see Galatians 5:6) God examines the motives of our hearts and knows when we are doing things to try to win the approval of other people, to put on a pious religious performance, to make a name for ourselves, or to take the easy road because we do not fully trust Him. As God's children, we inherently desire to be good and to do good things for Him, but sometimes our flesh and other desires wage war against our souls and cause us to do things that we do not want to do. (see 1 Peter 2:11; Romans 7:14-25) However, God supplies power for every deed that He prompts us to do as we listen to His voice and willingly obey Him, even if what He asks seems to be impossible. Moreover, at the end of the age when fire comes to test all of our works, it is only the good works that we have done which have been prompted by faith and genuine love that will pass through the test and receive a reward. (see 1 Corinthians 3:12-15, 13:13)

Through these things, Paul knew the name of Jesus would be glorified in believers and that believers would be glorified in Christ. *Glory* has to do with *honor, reverence, weightiness,* and *substance.* For example, when we respect someone because of who they are or the qualities we have seen in their lives, we give more weight to the things they say than we do the words of people for whom we have less respect. As we grow in holiness and are changed from the inside out to demonstrate the purity and goodness of Jesus through the things that we do and do not do, we cause others to take Him more seriously and give weight to the God that we serve because of what they see in us. Additionally, we share in Christ's glory as we suffer and endure through trials and tribulations in this world without succumbing to its ways. (see Romans 8:17; 1 Peter 4:14) We live our lives to follow Jesus because He brought more glory to God through His faith, love, and holiness than any of us ever will.

LIVE FREE BY GRACE (COLOSSIANS 1:9-14)

When Paul ministered at the church in Ephesus, he discipled a man named Epaphras. Then, Epaphras returned to his hometown of Colossae and when he shared the Gospel of Jesus Christ, the Colossian church was founded. Unfortunately, as the church grew, false teachings (and teachers) sprang up and diverted the attention of believers away from the purity of God's grace through faith in Jesus Christ alone. Colossae seemed to be a breeding ground for all sorts of wrong teachings which imposed rules and regulations on believers rather than trusting in God's grace alone. These teachings included those from a Jewish background that focused on religious observance of feasts, Sabbath days, abstention from certain foods and the like, and others which had more of a pagan origin in worship of spiritual beings, special knowledge, harsh piety, and the philosophies of men. (see Colossians 2:8-23) From prison, Paul wrote his letter to the believers at Colossae to give them solid and pure teaching of Christ's finished work and His supremacy above all other gods and forms of spirituality. Jesus has completely liberated us from all forms of religious legalism so that we are totally free to worship Him and live by faith.

This was Paul's prayer:

> *Colossians 1:9-14 - For this reason, since the day we heard about you, we have not stopped praying for you. We continually ask God to fill you with the knowledge of his will through all the wisdom and understanding that the Spirit gives, so that you may live a life worthy of the Lord and please him in every way: bearing fruit in every good work, growing in the knowledge of God, being strengthened with all power according to his glorious might so that you may have great endurance and patience, and giving joyful thanks to the Father, who has qualified you to share in the inheritance of his holy people in the kingdom of light. For he has rescued us from the dominion of darkness and brought us into the kingdom of the Son he loves, in whom we have redemption, the forgiveness of sins.*

Paul prayed for only one thing: that believers would be filled by the Holy Spirit with knowledge and understanding of God's will. Again, this *knowledge* and *spiritual wisdom* is *accurate understanding of God's divine nature* and *revelation* in the depths of our being with governing power for our lives. But this time, Paul emphasized not only knowing God but knowing His will. It is God's will for us to be totally free and unhindered by the things of this world and the schemes of man, religion, and the evil one because we know that we are loved by Him based exclusively on what Jesus has done for us. It is not God's will for us to beg for His approval through our words or our actions, thus negating and discounting the grace and love that He freely gives when we believe Him.

> *Galatians 5:1 - It is for freedom that Christ has set us free. Stand firm, then, and do not let yourselves be burdened again by a yoke of slavery.*

2 Corinthians 3:17 - Now the Lord is the Spirit, and where the Spirit of the Lord is, there is freedom.

This said, Paul desired for believers to live a life worthy of God and one that pleases Him. As we already discussed, our worthiness is proven only through our faith in Jesus, and it is also God's will for us to be holy and righteous in our conduct. This inherently means that He is not interested in any work we do that comes from a religious motivation. Putting on a piety performance, faking goodness, or even serving others while begrudging them in our hearts is the ultimate hypocrisy against God's grace and He is not fooled. (see Matthew 6:1-18) Using techniques and seeking after secret knowledge to reach higher spiritual realms is ridiculous when we consider the truth that we are already seated in Christ at the right hand of God in the highest heaven that there is. (see Colossians 2:8, 3:1; Revelation 2:24) Self-imposed standards of conduct, self-inflicted suffering as an act of devotion, and even mild self-deprecation as a form of feigned humility is a stench in the nose of God. Jesus was totally genuine; He did not strive to be heavenly and He never self-deprecated. He is God's beloved Son and He knows it confidently without a trace of arrogance. In the same way, as God's sons and daughters, who are we to enslave, beat up on, or insult what God loves and has deemed to be worthy of His love and freed by His grace? We cannot and should not try to earn what God has already freely given us by trying hard to be pleasing Him through our attempts to ascend higher or descend lower. (see Romans 10:6-7) We are pleasing to Him because of what Jesus did, and it is pleasing to Him when we trust in this sufficiency. To put it simply, if we are doing works to be good for God, then we are not actually doing the good works of God.

Colossians 2:22-23 - These rules, which have to do with things that are all destined to perish with use, are based on merely human commands and teachings. Such regulations indeed have an appearance of wisdom, with their self-imposed worship, their false humility and their harsh treatment of the body, but they lack any value in restraining sensual indulgence.

Ephesians 2:8-9 - For it is by grace you have been saved, through faith--and this is not from yourselves, it is the gift of God-- not by works, so that no one can boast.

Galatians 3:3 - Are you so foolish? After beginning by means of the Spirit, are you now trying to finish by means of the flesh?

Along these lines, Paul wanted believers to bear genuine fruit in every good work. Since before the foundation of the earth, God prepared good works for each one of us to do (see Ephesians 2:10), but only the Holy Spirit can guide us into doing them. For example, when Jesus walked on the earth, every time He entered the Temple there was a man who had been born lame sitting outside begging for alms. Even though Jesus healed many other lame people, He did not heal this one. Why? Because this was a good work reserved by God for Peter and John to do and which would open an opportunity for them to proclaim the Gospel of Jesus Christ to a crowd of thousands who would place their faith in Jesus. (see Acts 3:1-4:4) In the same way, there are times when God leads us not to do something that we think He would want us to do. We don't always know why; perhaps it is because He has prepared that particular good work for someone else or the person is simply not ready to receive from us yet. While we have no need for creating good works that we think God wants us to do, we also have no excuse for not following God's promptings to do things when He does speak to us. In fact, it makes it all the more important that we do obey His voice. In addition to this, we should always keep in mind that good works are not fruit. Spiritual fruitfulness and maturity is loving and blessing our enemies in the same way that we bless our friends and, in this, exhibiting the nature of Christ within us. (see Matthew 5:43-48)

Galatians 5:22-23 - But the fruit of the Spirit is love, joy, peace, forbearance, kindness, goodness, faithfulness, gentleness and self-control. Against such things there is no law.

God's perspective of our success in following Christ has very little to do with how many people we serve, preach to, or how many good things we do. Many people who do many "good" deeds, even miraculous and spiritual things in the name of the Lord, will not enter the Kingdom of Heaven but only those who do the will of God. (see Matthew 7:21-23) God gave His Son so that we can know Him personally. Through knowing Him, we become like Him. By being like Him, we stay in step with Him and do the good works that He has prepared for us.

Paul wanted our increased spiritual understanding of God and His will to strengthen us for endurance and patience as we are met with challenges in this world. Oftentimes, we pray for deliverance and a big fancy miracle solution to our problems, but God's desire is for our perseverance and trust in Him in the midst of chaos, confusion, and attack. This is because an unusual phenomenon occurs when we truly persist with the Lord in His will in spite of circumstances which appear to be the opposite of what He promised. Instead of our faith growing weaker, somehow it grows stronger. Trials give us experience with God's faithfulness, and this causes our hope of ultimate victory to increase. (see Romans 5:3-5) When we endure through tribulation instead of taking the easy escape route or placing our trust in something other than Jesus, we see first-hand how God moves things and people all around us to work for our benefit. We also experience the strength of His power within us to handle situations differently than we would without Him. In some Bible translations, *patience* is translated as *longsuffering*, which can also be known as suffering for a long time. While suffering is never fun and suffering for a long time is even less fun, as we persevere in waiting for God and all other solutions fade away or prove worthless, our faith in His power and ability rise up within us and overcome our desperation until we are fully persuaded of His good will toward us. (see Isaiah 40:31) In fact, longsuffering and perseverance is the very means by which we are brought to full spiritual maturity and Christlikeness if we will stand in faith and allow God to have His way with us.

> James 1:2-4 - *Consider it pure joy, my brothers and sisters, whenever you face trials of many kinds, because you know that the testing of your faith produces perseverance. Let perseverance finish its work so that you may be mature and complete, not lacking anything.*

For this reason, Paul intended for our knowledge of God to be coupled with constant and joyful thankfulness. The worst trial we will ever face is guaranteed to be God's biggest victory in our life. No matter what evil may be coming against us, and no matter how long we are called upon to endure and persevere, we can praise and thank God with confidence, knowing that He turns every curse into a blessing for us. Even in the midst of great trial, we do not have to turn to our own devices, religious acts, or the ways of this world in order to receive our deliverance from God. Instead, we can be thankful in everything we face because we trust that God is working it out for our good.

1 Thessalonians 5:18 - give thanks in all circumstances; for this is God's will for you in Christ Jesus.

For this reason, Paul closed his prayer with a reminder that *It is Finished!* Because of Jesus, we have been qualified for eternal life with God and heaven on earth. We have already been rescued out of the darkness of this world and all of its schemes and false impositions. We no longer have to feel inferior in any way for any reason, and we have no need of striving for dominance, money, or public success. Most importantly, we can cease from all worry about being good enough for God and from striving to complete religious acts to try to earn His approval or forgiveness. All our sins have been totally forgiven, all of the charges against us were nailed to the cross of Christ so that God never remembers them again, and every competing spiritual force in this world was completely humiliated and nullified through Jesus' sacrifice. (see Colossians 2:14-15) To lower ourselves to any other form of spirituality or restrict our lives with rule following is to fall from the grace that God has so freely extended to us. (see Galatians 5:4) We no longer have to follow rules or meet criteria to receive His love and be blessed. No matter what we have done in the past, what we are doing presently, or what we may do in the future, we are already totally free, completely loved, and absolutely accepted by God. In Christ, we have already been elevated to the highest spiritual position in all of creation and have been transferred to the Kingdom of Heaven as God's beloved children. May God's Kingdom come and His will to be done on earth as it is in Heaven! In Heaven, we worship our King who is worthy of our praise because He has done everything for us. There are no religious rules in Heaven.

REPENT & GROW TO MATURITY (2 CORINTHIANS 13:7-9)

Paul arrived in Corinth and preached the Gospel to Corinthian Jews until they rejected the message of Jesus being their Messiah. After this, he focused his attention on proclaiming the Good News to Corinthian Gentiles. He stayed in Corinth for a year and a half because the Lord spoke to him in a vision to tell him that many Corinthians would become believers. Eventually, the Jews there launched false accusations against Paul and brought him to court, only to have the charges dismissed by the Governor. Paul stayed in Corinth only a little while longer before wrapping up his second missionary journey and returning back to his home base in Antioch. (For more on Paul's time in Corinth, see Acts 18:1-18) The Corinthian believers embraced the Gospel message of freedom from sin and religion with zeal and enthusiasm. Unfortunately, they took it a little too far. These believers lived in a place that was so well-known for its unrestrained fornication that a Greek word *korinthiazomai,* which means *to act like a Corinthian,* was created as slang for engaging in wild sex. The Corinthians had placed their faith in Jesus but had failed to change their cultural way of life. To address this, Paul wrote a letter to the Corinthians (which has since been lost) while he was ministering in Ephesus on his third missionary journey. (see 1 Corinthians 5:9) The Corinthians did not alter their behavior but responded to Paul in a letter with many questions about the Christian faith and appropriate lifestyle for followers of Christ. From Ephesus, Paul wrote what we know of as 1 Corinthians as a response to them, bringing correction to their many errors. Even though the Corinthians were moving in gifts of the Holy Spirit when they assembled together, Paul could not address them as those who were mature in the Lord because their behavior clearly indicated that their lives were still ruled by their old fleshly nature and not by the Holy Spirit. (see 1 Corinthians 3:1-3) Jealousy, division, vanity, disorder, and sexual immorality were rampant among the believers, including a man who was sleeping with his father's wife. What's worse, the Corinthians boasted about it because of their knowledge of their freedom in Christ. (see 1 Corinthians 5:6) In addition, they were eating food offered to pagan gods, abusing the privilege and elements of communion, and were skeptical about the final resurrection. Unfortunately, the Corinthians did not receive Paul's letter very well because they did not want to change their way of doing things. Then, to make matters worse, some false teachers claiming to be apostles traveled through town slandering Paul, denying his apostolic authority, and insulting his non-intellectual approach to proclaiming the Gospel. At the same time, they tickled the ears of the Corinthians with teachings which did not require that they change any of their ways. For this reason, Paul made an unscheduled and brief trip to Corinth during the course of his third missionary journey but it was a "painful visit" because they openly rebelled against him and sided with the false apostles. After leaving town, Paul tearfully but authoritatively sent another letter to them (which has also since been lost) to severely address their errors and to warn them of God's coming judgment for the unrepentant. (see 2 Corinthians 2:1-4) Apparently, this letter penetrated the hearts of many Corinthians and they began to change their ways out of reverence for Christ. Nevertheless, the false apostles maligned Paul all the more. From Macedonia, Paul wrote 2 Corinthians to defend his position in their lives as the one who had originally shared the Gospel with them, to remind them of how he had always treated them with honesty and for their good, and how he never made any demands for money or repayment unlike the false apostles who abused them and wanted to be paid for it. (see 2 Corinthians 10-11) In spite of the fact that they were beginning to show signs of improvement, there was still much carnality among the Corinthian believers. Paul's only desire and prayer for them was for their faith to remain genuine so they could grow to maturity in the Lord.

This was Paul's prayer:

> *2 Corinthians 13:7-9 - Now we pray to God that you will not do anything wrong--not so that people will see that we have stood the test but so that you will do what is right even though we may seem to have failed. For we cannot do anything against the truth, but only for the truth. We are glad whenever we are weak but you are strong; and our prayer is that you may be fully restored.*

Without a hint of religious demand or condemnation, Paul prayed for believers to not do anything wrong but rather to do what was right. Christ has most definitely set us absolutely free from any and all condemnation for all of our sins and most of Paul's other prayers are aimed at bringing us into the full comprehension of this truth. However, knowledge of the unconditional love God for us is not intended to make us arrogant about our freedom to sin without eternal damnation. Rather, the freedom we have in Christ and the love and kindness of God toward us is intended to lead us to become the children of God and the new creations that we were born again to be through Christ's resurrection. (see 1 Corinthians 6:12, 8:1, 10:23) Our old self died on the cross so that we are no longer enslaved to our old nature and have no need to submit to its lusts in any area of our lives. Instead, we have the power and life of God within us to strengthen us so that we can offer ourselves as slaves of righteousness who do the godly thing and love others as Jesus loved us. (see Romans 6:18) We do not need to "clean up our act" in order to earn God's favor; we are already clean because of the Word of God and the blood of Jesus. (see John 15:3; 1 John 1:7) This said, because we are already clean, it is nonsensical for us to return to the filth of our old way of doing things. Our freedom from condemnation is designed by God to relieve us from the internal battle of doing what we do not want to do and not doing what we do want to do. (see Romans 7:14-8:1) Because nothing is forbidden (yes, truly nothing), the fear and the thrill of illicit defiance is dismantled. Therefore, when we sin, we are not heroes of Christian freedom but rather "like a dog returning to its vomit" or a "washed pig returning to the mud." (see 2 Peter 2:22; Proverbs 26:11)

Paul prayed for believers to be restored, using a Greek word that means *repaired, completed,* or *restored to proper condition,* and which is similar to *returning to good health after sickness.* Some translations phrase this to mean that Paul prayed for believers to grow to maturity. Maturity in the Christian life is to be like Jesus in all of His ways. Jesus maintained a deep abiding in the love of His Father at all times, He was pure and loving in all of His thoughts and actions towards others, and He worked miracles by the power of the Holy Spirit. Everything He did was for the purpose of revealing the heart of His Father to the world without dominating those who were weak or condemning those who were broken by sin. (see Matthew 12:18-20; Isaiah 42:3) The only thing He did that was cause for disbelief was to love us enough to die for us in spite of the fact that He is the King of all creation who could have judged and destroyed us. (see 1 Corinthians 1:23; Psalm 118:22) Our purpose, as His followers and as God's children, is to function from the same Spirit that

Jesus did in order to be the way He was and to lay down our lives for one another. (see 1 John 3:16) We take up our cross by trusting God and doing things in a way that honors Him rather than indulging our freedom from the Law with lawlessness that misrepresents God's wholesomeness or could sidetrack another person's pursuit of purity. (see 1 Corinthians 8, 10:23-32; Romans 14) Like Jesus, the only thing about our lives which should be a cause of confusion to everyone we encounter is how kind and gracious we are to one another, and even more so to those who hate us.

In addition to all of this, it is noteworthy that Paul's prayer was in no way an effort to prove his apostolic authority. All that mattered to him was for believers to have a genuine and personal faith in Christ and to live lives which evidenced the transforming power of God. Paul demonstrated that being a leader in the Church means being an expert *follower* of Jesus and walking in His ways as an example for others. (see 1 Corinthians 1:11) Instead of legitimizing ourselves in our own eyes and in the ways of this world with popularity, financial success, and the approval of masses, our faith and authority in the Lord is proven genuine through trials, persecution, and suffering for the name of Jesus. (see 2 Corinthians 4:8-12, 6:3-13, 11:16-33) God's supernatural love is revealed in and through our lives when we build one another up instead of tearing one another down, manipulating one another for our own agendas, or peddling spirituality for profit. Being an intellectual expert to outsmart one another and display how much we know about God amounts to nothing when it is compared to unpretentious childlike faith and dependence on God which demonstrates that we actually know Him. Paul exhorted believers to examine our own faith to see if we truly believe all that Christ died to give us. (see 2 Corinthians 13:5-6) We know that our faith is genuine by how the power of God is being revealed through the lives that we live.

The forces of this world and the lusts of our flesh are constantly at work seeking to steer us away from the simplicity of devotion to Christ. God gives us power through the Holy Spirit to walk in paths of righteousness, and He does so in order for the name of Jesus and His reputation to be glorified in the earth. (see Psalm 23:3) May our lives be demonstrations of our sincere faith in all that He has done for us and may our faith be demonstrated through our genuine *agape* love.

CHAPTER FOUR
BLESSINGS FOR THE RIGHTEOUS

MY GOAL IS THAT THEY MAY BE ENCOURAGED IN
HEART AND UNITED IN LOVE, SO THAT THEY MAY
HAVE THE FULL RICHES OF COMPLETE
UNDERSTANDING, IN ORDER THAT THEY MAY
KNOW THE MYSTERY OF GOD, NAMELY, CHRIST, IN
WHOM ARE HIDDEN ALL THE TREASURES OF
WISDOM AND KNOWLEDGE.
– THE APOSTLE PAUL, COLOSSIANS 2:2-3

Throughout Paul's letters, he continually prayed blessings upon believers. He knew all too well that it is the kindness of God and His undeserved blessings which humble us in our attitudes and way of seeing things while drawing us closer to the heart of God and conforming us to the likeness of Christ. (see Romans 2:4)

Paul's approach completely reflects the central purpose of Jesus' ministry on earth. Jesus came to make a way for those who place our faith in Him to have access to Heaven for ourselves both now and for eternity. His core message was, "Repent for the Kingdom of Heaven is at hand!" To *repent* means to *change one's mind, reverse one's decision about something, to think differently, or to reconsider*. This means that Jesus was essentially saying, "Change your mind; believe that God loves you so much that He sent Me, and righteousness, peace, and joy in the Holy Spirit are yours now." This is really GOOD NEWS! This said, to anyone who considers God to be unforgiving, mean, angry, or punitive, Good News is totally unexpected and requires a complete transformation of our thinking about who God is and what He desires to do for us. Sometimes, it even means we have to admit that we have been wrong about God or about Jesus for a very long time.

Our repentance when we first believe that Jesus is Lord is probably the most significant moment of our lives and is one over which the angels of heaven rejoice. (see Luke 15:7, 10) However, repentance in the Christian life never ends until we are fully mature and entirely like Jesus. As we allow the Holy Spirit to work in our lives, He changes our perspective on just about everything.

> *Romans 12:2 - Do not conform to the pattern of this world, but be transformed by the renewing of your mind. Then you will be able to test and approve what God's will is--his good, pleasing and perfect will.*

The Holy Spirit works within us to renovate our thoughts, feelings, purposes, and desires. When these things are aligned with the heart of God, we discern good and evil, have strength to do His will, and even have power to bring Heaven to earth as proof of His grace and goodness toward us who believe His Son. (see Hebrews 5:14; Matthew 6:10) However, being awakened to the truth that God is a loving Father rather than a harsh Master, and that His love and blessings for us as His children are available for free through faith in Jesus, is a real shock to our fleshly instincts and a total affront to the ways of this world and every form of religion. In fact, it means that the things we thought we needed to do to survive, succeed, and be blessed are a total waste of time and energy because they have no value in the sight of God. (see Isaiah 55:1-3, 64:6; Matthew 11:28-30; John 6:29)

This makeover of our entire approach to God and to life here on earth is called sanctification. To be *sanctified* is to be *clean, pure,* and *free from guilt through complete atonement.* By the blood of Jesus, believers **were** totally sanctified through His sacrifice, and we **become** sanctified as we allow the Holy Spirit to work in our hearts to cleanse and purify us. This means that in God's sight we are already washed, cleansed, and purified, and the Holy Spirit works within us to change our way of thinking until our thoughts and actions are a reflection of the way that God already sees us. Or, you could say that our sanctification in Christ is the process of becoming what we already are.

> *Hebrews 10:10, 14 - And by that will, we have been made holy through the sacrifice of the body of Jesus Christ once for all. ... For by one sacrifice he has made perfect forever those who are being made holy.*

> *John 17:17, 19 - Sanctify them by the truth; your word is truth. ... For them I sanctify myself, that they too may be truly sanctified.*

Practically speaking, only those who are sanctified have right standing with God or are, in a word, righteous. And, only those who are righteous have a right to God's blessings. For this reason, the mind boggling, transformative, repentance-inducing Good News is that through our faith in Christ, we are now righteous in God's sight and, therefore, we are able to receive all of the blessings that are only available to righteous people.[2] God's kindness and goodness abound toward us simply because we believe Jesus and what He did for us. Wow! Hallelujah! Praise the Lord! This is beyond exciting! In fact, this is so astounding and so important for us to understand that it is the central and almost single-minded intent of most of Paul's blessings and prayers. Paul prayed, in essence, for those who are already righteous in God's sight to come into alignment with God's good will for us.

Two more quick things before we jump into Paul's blessings…First of all, Paul often blessed believers as a greeting or farewell or by saying, *"May God…"*, which is the same as saying, *"I pray that God will…"* This is seen frequently in the Scriptures as a confirmation or proclamation of what the speaker knows to be God's will. For example, the first person to pray in this way was Noah when He prophetically declared God's will regarding what would happen in the lives of his three sons and their descendants and then, it came to pass just as Noah said. (see Genesis 9:27) In the same way, Paul confirmed God's will for everyone who believes Jesus to be blessed and declared God's blessing to them in his

---

[2] For some (but certainly not all) blessings for the righteous, see: Psalms 23, 34, 37, 91, 92, 103, 112, 118 and Proverbs 10, 11, 12, 13.

letters. Secondly, in his blessings, Paul made different requests to the Father, the Son, and the Holy Spirit. To be clear, there is only one God, and God is One. (see Deuteronomy 6:4) The Father is God, the Son is God, and the Holy Spirit is God. All three work together according to God's will, but within God's will they each have unique roles and functions in the lives of disciples and on the earth. Here is a general guideline: Calling upon the Father results in a spiritual drawing towards redemption and restoration through a flood of endless love coupled with pure wisdom and justice. Entreating the Son pulls upon and brings into effect a fathomless mercy, a compassion that heals, and virtuous guidance from our eternal Shepherd. Appealing to the Holy Spirit leads to divine revelation of truth for purification and freedom, comfort and assurance of God's goodness, and power from heaven for Kingdom purposes. They each work toward the same objective, which is for everyone to have eternal life by knowing the Father through faith in the Son in order to become His sons and daughters. Regardless of how Paul arranged his words, and which One of the Godhead the blessings were addressed to, they all highlight God's goodness toward us who believe His Son, Jesus.

GRACE & PEACE

Paul repeatedly blessed believers with grace and peace. He did this as often as he could, oftentimes at the beginning and close of his letters, in order to perpetually remind us of God's good will toward us no matter what the conditions in this world or circumstances in our lives may seem to indicate. I realize that listing all of these may be overdoing it, but I do so in order to express how much Paul reiterated and restated God's heart of grace and peace again and again so that we might finally believe, to the depths of our souls, in His abounding goodness toward us.

These were Paul's blessings:

> *Romans 1:7 - To all in Rome who are loved by God and called to be his holy people: Grace and peace to you from God our Father and from the Lord Jesus Christ.*

> *Romans 15:13 - May the God of hope fill you with all joy and peace as you trust in him, so that you may overflow with hope by the power of the Holy Spirit.*

Romans 16:20 - The God of peace will soon crush Satan under your feet. The grace of our Lord Jesus be with you.

1 Corinthians 1:2-3 - To the church of God in Corinth, to those sanctified in Christ Jesus and called to be his holy people, together with all those everywhere who call on the name of our Lord Jesus Christ--their Lord and ours: Grace and peace to you from God our Father and the Lord Jesus Christ.

1 Corinthians 16:23 - The grace of the Lord Jesus be with you.

2 Corinthians 1:2 - Grace and peace to you from God our Father and the Lord Jesus Christ.

2 Corinthians 13:14 - May the grace of the Lord Jesus Christ, and the love of God, and the fellowship of the Holy Spirit be with you all.

Galatians 1:3-5 - Grace and peace to you from God our Father and the Lord Jesus Christ, who gave himself for our sins to rescue us from the present evil age, according to the will of our God and Father, to whom be glory for ever and ever. Amen.

Galatians 6:18 - The grace of our Lord Jesus Christ be with your spirit, brothers and sisters. Amen.

Ephesians 1:2 - Grace and peace to you from God our Father and the Lord Jesus Christ.

Ephesians 6:23-24 - Peace to the brothers and sisters, and love with faith from God the Father and the Lord Jesus Christ. Grace to all who love our Lord Jesus Christ with an undying love.

Philippians 1:2 - Grace and peace to you from God our Father and the Lord Jesus Christ.

Philippians 4:23 - The grace of the Lord Jesus Christ be with your spirit. Amen.

Colossians 1:2 - To God's holy people in Colossae, the faithful brothers and sisters in Christ: Grace and peace to you from God our Father.

Colossians 4:18 - I, Paul, write this greeting in my own hand.

Remember my chains. Grace be with you.

1 Thessalonians 1:1 - Paul, Silas and Timothy, To the church of the Thessalonians in God the Father and the Lord Jesus Christ: Grace and peace to you.

1 Thessalonians 5:28 - The grace of our Lord Jesus Christ be with you.

2 Thessalonians 1:2 - Grace and peace to you from God the Father and the Lord Jesus Christ.

2 Thessalonians 3:16, 18 - Now may the Lord of peace himself give you peace at all times and in every way. The Lord be with all of you. ... The grace of our Lord Jesus Christ be with you all.

1 Timothy 1:2 - To Timothy my true son in the faith: Grace, mercy and peace from God the Father and Christ Jesus our Lord.

1 Timothy 6:21b - Grace be with you all.

2 Timothy 1:2 - To Timothy, my dear son: Grace, mercy and peace from God the Father and Christ Jesus our Lord.

2 Timothy 4:22 - The Lord be with your spirit. Grace be with you all.

Titus 1:4 - To Titus, my true son in our common faith: Grace and peace from God the Father and Christ Jesus our Savior.

Titus 3:15b - Grace be with you all.

Philemon 1:3 - Grace and peace to you from God our Father and the Lord Jesus Christ.

Philemon 1:25 - The grace of the Lord Jesus Christ be with your spirit.

Paul blessed believers with grace and peace twenty-seven times in thirteen letters because he desperately wanted us to grasp the infinite love and kindness of God for us in Christ. Could he have made God's goodness toward us any clearer?

God's grace has to do with the favorable treatment that we receive because of His delight in us as His righteous ones. This means that we are given preferred status, special courtesies, blessings, kindnesses, advancements, and even our mistakes and wrong choices are worked out for our good because we are loved by God who is sovereign over everything. We are loved and blessed by God simply because He loves to bless us! The reason we need to be reminded of God's grace so repeatedly is because deep down we know that we deserve nothing from God except His judgment and the full penalty for everything that we have ever done wrong. But now, simply because we believe Jesus, God's judgments are always in our favor, no matter what we have done. This makes no sense! In fact, it would be an absolute atrocity against justice if Jesus had not taken all of the judgment against us upon Himself. But because Jesus received the judgment that we deserved, we receive every good thing that we do not deserve. We are perpetually established in God's good graces, no matter what we have done, are doing, or will do.

Similarly, peace is not simply lack of war, chaos, or confusion although it does include this. The blessing of peace, which Paul with his Jewish heritage was undoubtedly bestowing upon believers, is shalom peace. *Shalom* includes *wholeness, safety, soundness, wellness, prosperity, health, contentment, friendship*, and the *perfect harmony* that comes only when each individual part is functioning to its fullest capacity together with every other part. Again, inherently we know that we deserve the utter chaos, broken relationships, disease, and discord as the consequences for all the wrong choices we have made in our lives. However, Jesus as our Prince of Peace gives us free access to all of the benefits of shalom in addition to peace with God—a kind of peace that the world simply cannot offer. (see Isaiah 9:6; John 14:27) Because of this, no matter what is going on in the world around us, we can rest assured that unfavorable circumstances are no longer an indication that God is displeased with us. God is not punishing us because ALL of our punishment was laid upon Jesus on the cross. For this reason, we can be confident that it is God's will for us to be blessed with total shalom, all the time.

Along these lines and in these blessings, Paul also blessed believers with joy. True biblical joy is a calm delight and gladness that pervades our lives until we glow and radiate with contentment, no matter what is happening in our lives. As an illustration, an unweaned child panics and pouts at the slightest twinge of hunger, desperately grasping for sustenance out of urgent fear. But a weaned child is settled and secure and can enjoy every moment of the day without worry or fret because they trust that what they need will be provided at just the right time. (see Psalm 131:1-2) In the same way, as God's children, He desires for us to be able to enjoy everything that we do being soothed, unselfish, and unbothered because we are totally confident that He is truly working on our behalf and working for our good. We don't have to strive or agonize about anything because we know that our Heavenly Father is faithful and good.

In these blessings, Paul also gave an honorable mention to God's mercy, love, hope, and fellowship with the Holy Spirit, which we have touched upon in other chapters. Mercy is not receiving the punishment that we deserve, even when we stumble and fail to reflect God's perfection. Love is God's unconditional charitable disposition toward us, His endless patience with us, kindness towards us, and willingness to be good to us even when we use our free will in error. Hope is confident expectation of good and absolute trust that God will fulfill every promise He has made to us, both in this age and the age to come. Fellowship with the Holy Spirit is partnership, cooperation, and co-laboring with God through which we mature spiritually, exhibit the fruit of the Spirit, and fulfill God's plans in the earth.

God's grace, peace, and all of His blessings are ours in abundance because we believe in what Jesus has done for us. We need to be continually and repeatedly reminded of this because the more we really believe it, the more we are able receive it and even see the fruit of it in our lives.

STRENGTH, COURAGE, PURITY, UNITY

Part of the reason why Paul desired for believers to be perpetually and fully assured of God's undying love for us in Christ is because even as followers of Jesus and beloved children of God, we will still face many trials and tribulations while we are here on the earth. (see John 16:33; Acts 14:22) In fact, the world hates our guts. (see John 15:18-20, 17:14; Matthew 10:22) Being a child of God is not a *get-out-of-problems-free* pass and, oftentimes, it seems that the most faithful followers encounter some of the most challenging trials of faith.

In line with this, Paul asked God to bless believers with everything needed for spiritual endurance. Interestingly, he prayed four out of five of this type of blessing for the Thessalonians who faced brutally intense persecution against their Christian faith by their fellow countrymen.

These were Paul's prayers for them:

> *1 Thessalonians 3:12-13 - May the Lord make your love increase and overflow for each other and for everyone else, just as ours does for you. May he strengthen your hearts so that you will be blameless and holy in the presence of our God and Father when our Lord Jesus comes with all his holy ones.*

> *1 Thessalonians 5:23-24 - May God himself, the God of peace, sanctify you through and through. May your whole spirit, soul and body be kept blameless at the coming of our Lord Jesus Christ. The one who calls you is faithful, and he will do it.*

> *2 Thessalonians 2:16-17 - May our Lord Jesus Christ himself and God our Father, who loved us and by his grace gave us eternal encouragement and good hope, encourage your hearts and strengthen you in every good deed and word.*

> *2 Thessalonians 3:5 - May the Lord direct your hearts into God's love and Christ's perseverance.*

No matter what the world, the flesh, or the devil may throw against us, we have to know who we are as God's children and that He is constantly pouring out His grace and peace to us. Otherwise, we may look at our sin, our circumstances, or the brokenness of this world and allow ourselves to be deceived into believing that our sins are not fully forgiven or that God does not love us and have good will towards us. The original deceptive play made by the evil one in the Garden of Eden was to convince Adam and Eve that God was keeping them from good things rather than being the only source of every good thing. (see Genesis 3) The enemy's tactics haven't changed except that, these days, he does not slither up to us as an actual serpent but exhibits himself through our trials.

When we encounter hardship, persecution, or various other miseries and maladies, it tests the core of what we truly believe about God's disposition toward us. Trials have a voice that asks if we will still believe that God loves us, even when it seems to be more evident in what we are experiencing that He does not. Suffering forces us to decide between trusting God and His power or taking things into our own hands by exerting our strength to bring about the outcome we desire. Our motives and self-justifications are laid bare and reveal just how much we truly trust God. We either choose to trust God and His ways, or we choose to trust in ourselves and the ways of this world.

> *1John 2:15-16 NLT - Do not love this world nor the things it offers you, for when you love the world, you do not have the love of the Father in you. For the world offers only a craving for physical pleasure, a craving for everything we see, and pride in our achievements and possessions. These are not from the Father, but are from this world.*

For this reason, Paul asked God to bless believers with encouragement that gives strength to trust in Jesus and to continue in God's way of doing things. This requires faith and endurance. It is harder to trust an invisible God to work on our behalf than it is to take control and trust in ourselves. It is more difficult to place higher value on eternal rewards for doing things the right way than it is to procure temporal benefits for ourselves through the use of our own methods. It is challenging to obey God when His path of life seems to lead toward death. It can seem absurd to continue in self-denial when it apparently leads to more and more misery, particularly over a prolonged period of time.

This said, it is this kind of faith that keeps us truly blameless in what we do. It is one thing to suffer for doing right, but it is altogether different when we suffer for doing something wrong. (see 1 Peter 3:13-17) When we make wrong choices, God in His goodness works on our behalf to cause it to work out for our good. However, there is a certain value in being truly innocent and having a genuinely clear conscience before God and man. In fact, this is true whether or not we are enduring a trial. The desires of our flesh and for the things of this world are always in contrast to the will of God and cause us to try to find our own way out of difficulty to end our suffering, take the path of least resistance by pleasing people or following the pattern of this world, or pursue temporal rewards rather than eternal ones. But, the Holy Spirit is always at work to keep us from indulging in impure pursuits if we will submit ourselves to His guidance.

Simply put, when we know God's love and good will toward us, we trust Him. When we trust Him, we have no fear. When we have no fear, we give no place to wrong motives. When we have no wrong motives, we do not sin. (see 1 John 3:6-9, 4:16-18) When this purity is worked into our hearts, we are more useful to God for good works. (see 2 Timothy 2:20-21) Through all of this, we exhibit God's love and good nature through the things we say and do for every onlooker and witness to see. When this happens, we testify of Jesus even without words.

The fifth of Paul's blessings of this type was written to the Roman Christians who were dealing with conflicts and issues of disunity within their church. This group of believers included many Jewish followers of Jesus who had previously been expelled from Rome by Emperor Claudius in 49 A.D. and who had only recently been allowed to return to Rome by the time Paul wrote his letter to them in 57 A.D. There was serious tension between these returned Jewish believers and the Gentile Christians who had continued the church in Rome during their absence. While the Thessalonians' trials had caused their love for one another to grow even deeper, the Roman believers were struggling to keep peace with one another.

This was Paul's prayer:

> *Romans 15:5-6 - May the God who gives endurance and encouragement give you the same attitude of mind toward each other that Christ Jesus had, so that with one mind and one voice you may glorify the God and Father of our Lord Jesus Christ.*

From every nation, tribe, and tongue on the earth (Jew and Gentile equally and alike), God has redeemed a people for Himself to be a chosen generation, a royal priesthood, and the holy nation of God. (see

Revelation 5:9; 1 Peter 2:9) In God's eternal perspective, one generation of man is descended from Adam, whom He created back in the beginning. Another generation of man was born again through the resurrection of Christ to be children not of Adam, but of God. We who believe Jesus are now a whole different kind of people on the earth and this means we have everything that matters in common with one another as God's chosen ones! (see Acts 2:44, 4:32; Galatians 6:15)

For this reason, Paul prayed for God to bless believers with the same mindset toward one another that Jesus has toward us. When we forget that we have been made one with one another through our faith in Christ, we give place to the evil one and disharmony sets in. (see Ephesians 4:26) Generally speaking, divisions in the church are rooted in jealousy, selfish ambition, the love of money, and following anyone other than Jesus. (see James 3:15-16; 1 Timothy 6:10; 1 Corinthians 1:11-12, 3:4-5) When these things are present or tolerated, they lead to judgmentalism, superiority, and domination, which take over and wreak havoc. In contrast, Jesus prayed for all of His followers to be united as one with one another and showed us the way to bring this oneness into reality. (see John 17:11, 21, 23) When we were His enemies, He died for us. When we deserved wrath, He showed mercy. When we had nothing, He gave us everything. (see Romans 5:8; Colossians 1:21-22; 2 Corinthians 8:9) He never judged or condemned, but rather He saved, healed, and delivered without cost to the guilty. (see John 3:17, 12:47; Matthew 10:8) Everything He did was for the purpose of revealing His Father so that everyone who would believe could have eternal life.

To put it plainly, Jesus was a foot washer. If we as His followers really understand what He did for us, then we will take the lowest place and humble ourselves before God to do the lowliest things for other people rather than assert our rights and demand our desires. Through this, our supernatural strength, courage, peace, and unity with one another demonstrate to the world that we are truly His.

FAITH, LOVE, FRUIT OF THE GOSPEL

At times in Paul's letters, he praised God for the various ways believers were already demonstrating that the truth of the Gospel and the goodness of God were penetrating deep into their lives. Paul used his God-given authority to build believers up by highlighting, emphasizing, and encouraging the good things they were successfully putting into practice.

These were some of Paul's praises:

> *1 Thessalonians 1:2-3 - We always thank God for all of you and continually mention you in our prayers. We remember before our God and Father your work produced by faith, your labor prompted by love, and your endurance inspired by hope in our Lord Jesus Christ.*

> *1 Thessalonians 3:9 - How can we thank God enough for you in return for all the joy we have in the presence of our God because of you?*

> *2 Thessalonians 1:3 - We ought always to thank God for you, brothers and sisters, and rightly so, because your faith is growing more and more, and the love all of you have for one another is increasing.*

> *Philemon 1:4-5 - I always thank my God as I remember you in my prayers, because I hear about your love for all his holy people and your faith in the Lord Jesus.*

Paul praised the believers who were exhibiting their faith through their love for one another. As followers of Jesus, we are called to live our lives in such a way that we demonstrate our understanding of the grace and peace of our Father in Heaven and our gratitude to Him for it by extending His grace and peace to others as well. (see Galatians 5:6) If we say that we believe Jesus but we do not reveal it in the things that we do, then we are self-deceived. (see James 2:18; 1 John 4:20) Our actions speak for themselves, and their voice is louder than thousands of words could ever be. Our love proves our faith.

These were more of Paul's praises:

> *Colossians 1:3-6 - We always thank God, the Father of our Lord Jesus Christ, when we pray for you, because we have heard of your faith in Christ Jesus and of the love you have for all God's people-- the faith and love that spring from the hope stored up*

for you in heaven and about which you have already heard in the true message of the gospel that has come to you. In the same way, the gospel is bearing fruit and growing throughout the whole world--just as it has been doing among you since the day you heard it and truly understood God's grace.

1 Thessalonians 2:13 - And we also thank God continually because, when you received the word of God, which you heard from us, you accepted it not as a human word, but as it actually is, the word of God, which is indeed at work in you who believe.

2 Thessalonians 2:13 - But we ought always to thank God for you, brothers and sisters loved by the Lord, because God chose you as firstfruits to be saved through the sanctifying work of the Spirit and through belief in the truth.

1 Corinthians 1:4-7 - I always thank my God for you because of his grace given you in Christ Jesus. For in him you have been enriched in every way--with all kinds of speech and with all knowledge-- God thus confirming our testimony about Christ among you. Therefore you do not lack any spiritual gift as you eagerly wait for our Lord Jesus Christ to be revealed.

Philippians 1:4-6 - In all my prayers for all of you, I always pray with joy because of your partnership in the gospel from the first day until now, being confident of this, that he who began a good work in you will carry it on to completion until the day of Christ Jesus.

Romans 1:8 - First, I thank my God through Jesus Christ for all of you, because your faith is being reported all over the world.

Paul praised God for the ways that it was plain to see that the power of God was at work in the lives of believers. The Gospel is the power of God to transform lives. (see Romans 1:16) This means that where the simple Gospel of Jesus Christ who died to save sinners is proclaimed, God's power will be evident through repentance, generosity, love, and enduring change in the lives of those who hear it and even by the supernatural manifestations for miracles, signs, and wonders. (see Hebrews 4:6; Mark 16:20) The same power that raised Jesus from the dead dwells within us to strengthen and empower us to know and to do the will of God, and to bring the Kingdom of Heaven to the earth as proof that Jesus is the one and only Son of God and the Lord over all creation. The world takes note, and the Gospel is proclaimed not only in our words but also through our lives.

PRAYER AT ALL TIMES

Paul's desire was for believers to experience the fullness of all that Jesus died to give us. For this reason, he devoted his life to prayer and prayed for believers continually.

2 Timothy 1:3 - I thank God, whom I serve, as my ancestors did, with a clear conscience, as night and day I constantly remember you in my prayers.

Romans 1:9-10a - God, whom I serve in my spirit in preaching the gospel of his Son, is my witness how constantly I remember you in my prayers at all times;

Ephesians 1:16 - I have not stopped giving thanks for you, remembering you in my prayers.

Colossians 1:9 - For this reason, since the day we heard about you, we have not stopped praying for you. We continually ask God to fill you with the knowledge of his will through all the wisdom and understanding that the Spirit gives,

1 Thessalonians 3:10 - Night and day we pray most earnestly that we may see you again and supply what is lacking in your faith.

2 Thessalonians 1:11 - With this in mind, we constantly pray for you, that our God may make you worthy of his calling, and that by his power he may bring to fruition your every desire for goodness and your every deed prompted by faith.

Paul knew all too well that being transformed by the power of God and serving the Lord is a full-time endeavor. Each follower of Jesus has a unique journey to spiritual maturity, which requires maintaining constant communication with the Lord. So, Paul urged believers to follow his example and enter into a lifestyle that is devoted to prayer.

Colossians 4:2 - Devote yourselves to prayer, being watchful and thankful.

Philippians 4:6 - Do not be anxious about anything, but in every situation, by prayer and petition, with thanksgiving, present your requests to God.

Ephesians 6:18 - And pray in the Spirit on all occasions with all kinds of prayers and requests. With this in mind, be alert and always keep on praying for all the Lord's people.

Paul's encouragement was the same as what Jesus taught His disciples about prayer. Jesus encouraged His disciples to keep on asking, seeking, and knocking until we fully receive, find, and enter into the fullness of all that God has for us. (see Matthew 7:7-8) One of Jesus' parables about prayer was about a widow who, no matter how long it took, would not give up on petitioning the judge for the justice that was rightfully due her until she received it. (see Luke 18:1-8) Another of His prayer parables was about an impertinent friend who came at an inappropriate time to ask for something that he needed in order to give it to someone else. In this parable, the request is granted not because of the asker's impertinence, but for the sake of the reputation of the giver who was known to possess the needed thing. (see Luke 11:5-8) Through these teachings, Jesus encouraged His followers to devote our lives to persistent prayer, to know what is rightfully ours in Him, and to trust that God will supply all that we need even if it is sometimes only for the sake of His own reputation as the one true God who created and owns everything.

In addition to this, prayer is a private thing and is best done alone in the secret place with the Lord and is not a flashy thing to be put on display as a boast. We should refrain from praying from a motive of being praised by people for our eloquence, knowledge of God, or how much Scripture we can quote. (see Matthew 6:5-8) This said, it can be encouraging to our brothers and sisters in the Lord when we reassure them that we are praying for them and it is okay to tell them so as long as we truly are praying for them. When Paul demonstrated this in some of his letters, it was not to boast about his prayers or show off his great theological prowess. Instead, he demonstrated to the disciples, who looked to him for guidance, that he was dependent on God for everything just like we are and that only the Lord can answer any of our prayers.

All of this is to say again that repentance is not a one-time event in the Christian life but a never-ending journey of discovering God's goodness. God desires for us to be reminded again and again of His bottomless love, grace, and peace until we finally believe that Heaven is ours both now and in the age to come. His goodness transforms us from the inside out into righteous and sanctified children of God who reveal our Father's love to the world. So, starting today, change your mind; believe that God loves you because of Jesus and Heaven can be yours now here on earth.

CHAPTER FIVE

FOR LABORERS

FOR WHEN I PREACH THE GOSPEL, I CANNOT
BOAST, SINCE I AM COMPELLED TO PREACH. WOE
TO ME IF I DO NOT PREACH THE GOSPEL!
– THE APOSTLE PAUL, 1 CORINTHIANS 9:16

The Apostle Paul was probably the most effective co-laborer with God that the world has ever known. This said, he knew that his endeavors were greatly helped by the prayers of believers everywhere and for this reason, he often requested prayer for himself in his letters to the churches. Interestingly, the only thing Jesus told His disciples to pray for other than the Lord's prayer was for laborers in God's harvest field.

> *Matthew 9:37-38 NKJV - Then He said to His disciples, "The harvest truly [is] plentiful, but the laborers [are] few. "Therefore pray the Lord of the harvest to send out laborers into His harvest."*

Through Paul's prayers and prayer requests for himself, we have a glimpse into how to pray for God's laborers today.

A SERVANT OF THE LORD

First and foremost, Paul knew that he was a servant of the Lord. He began his letters by identifying himself as a servant of God or an apostle of Jesus Christ by the will of God. Paul used the same word for servant or bond-servant that is used to describe a slave or one who is totally owned and committed to one Master. An apostle is a messenger or delegate who has been sent with orders from someone else as that person's representative. Paul knew that he was carrying out Jesus' business for God's purposes and only by God's will.

Galatians 1:1 - Paul, an apostle--sent not from men nor by a man, but by Jesus Christ and God the Father, who raised him from the dead—

Paul could not have been any clearer that he was a servant of God and not a servant of man. He was appointed by God, sent by God, and accountable to God alone as the final authority regarding his success or failure. Paul did not bow down to the demands of anyone and his service was not initiated or compelled by people's needs or trying to win their approval. This is because it is impossible to seek the approval of men and the approval of God at the same time. Compromising the true message of Christ in the interest of appealing to more people is only a cowardly retreat from the persecution that results when Jesus is revealed as He really is. (see Galatians 1:10, 6:12; John 5:44)

Paul also never boasted in his apostleship and did not regard it as a title for domineering. Because Paul had been an aggressive persecutor of Christians before his life-changing encounter with the Lord, he knew to the depths of his being that he had the privilege of serving Christ only because of God's unfathomable mercy and undeserved favor. In fact, sometimes it seems that God chooses and sends those who will be the most offensive and baffling among the audience to which He sends them. He does things like sending his Son to be born in a feeding trough, sending out uneducated fishermen to proclaim the Scriptures to religious experts, and transforming the most religious, judgmental, Law-following taskmasters into a messenger of grace, unconditional love, and freely-given blessings. Personally, I believe that God does it this way in order to expose the offense and reveal the heart of those who are listening so as to swiftly uncover what they are truly placing their faith in under the surface. (see James 2:18) Nevertheless, God uses vessels that demonstrate His power, mercy, and grace, and bring Him glory through their dependence on Him and by freely giving out what they have freely received from Him.

Secondly, Paul knew that God's purpose for him was to proclaim the Gospel of Jesus Christ to all people and to nurture the growth of all believers to spiritual maturity in in the Lord.

Romans 1:1-5 - Paul, a servant of Christ Jesus, called to be an apostle and set apart for the gospel of God-- the gospel he promised beforehand through his prophets in the Holy Scriptures regarding his Son, who as to his earthly life was a descendant of David, and who through the Spirit of holiness was appointed the Son of God in power by his resurrection from the dead: Jesus Christ our Lord. Through him we received grace and apostleship to call all the Gentiles to the obedience that comes from faith for his name's sake.

Titus 1:1-3 - Paul, a servant of God and an apostle of Jesus Christ to further the faith of God's elect and their knowledge of the truth that leads to godliness-- in the hope of eternal life, which God, who does not lie, promised before the beginning of time, and which now at his appointed season he has brought to light through the preaching entrusted to me by the command of God our Savior,

2 Timothy 1:1 NLT - This letter is from Paul, chosen by the will of God to be an apostle of Christ Jesus. I have been sent out to tell others about the life he has promised through faith in Christ Jesus.

God's heart and eternal plan of redemption for mankind had been worked into every fiber of Paul's being. Actually, by definition, this is what being a co-laborer is. The Greek word for *co-laborer* is *synergos*, like our word for synergy. In my days as a ballet dancer, when two or more of us were so entirely in sync with one another that there seemed to be a special extra *something* added to our dancing, we called it *synergy*. In a way, this is what co-laboring with God for His Kingdom is like. We do not work for God by serving Him through our own ideas and initiative. We must be willing to be led by Jesus into His plans, in His timing, and in His way of doing things in order to be in sync with His heart so as to carry out His work. When we do this, He adds a special grace to our lives and a blessing to the work of our hands. This is also true when we co-labor with one another. Timothy and Titus had spent so much time with Paul that they were commended for having the same heart and spirit as Paul and even behaving in the same way that Paul did towards people. (see Philippians 2:20; 2 Corinthians 12:18) And yet, even though Timothy and Titus were sent by Paul on assignments with instructions from him, on a deeper level they were each individually sent by God and dependent on God alone.

Until Jesus returns, we are called to co-labor with God and with one another towards the fulfillment of His redemptive plan for mankind. We are soldiers in a war that is not of this world as the kingdom of darkness contends aggressively against us as the light of the world and calls us into battles of good versus evil, hope versus despair, and faith in eternal life versus the fear of death. We are in this together as God's co-laborers and we need to encourage one another to persist in believing God's goodness, walking in His love, and fulfilling our role as ambassadors of Heaven.

Actually, as servants whose Kingdom is not of this world, Paul exhorted that we not become entangled in worldly pursuits of any kind which drain the time, energy, and resources that we could be using for God's Kingdom. (see 2 Timothy 2:4) Jesus never prayed about or involved Himself in activist causes or in world politics while He was on earth even though His fellow countrymen wanted a Messiah who would do so and take over the world on their behalf. The only time that Jesus met with kings and rulers of this world was during the trial leading up to His crucifixion and He did not talk much. He was singularly focused on the Kingdom of God. Paul went so far as to say that he wished that everyone were unmarried in order for us to be undivided in our interests and unburdened by worldly responsibilities. (see 1 Corinthians 7:7) Although Paul conceded that singleness for everyone was not possible in this age, it certainly expresses just how single-mindedly he wanted believers to be focused on the Kingdom of God and His purposes.

Paul also warned in some of his letters that true servants of the Lord must not be argumentative. (see 2 Timothy 2:24) Engaging in unnecessary controversies over worldly things or even the things of God ruins the faith of those who are listening. For this reason, Paul encouraged believers to avoid divisive people. (see 1 Timothy 6:20; Titus 3:9-10) People were quite divided in their views about Jesus, but He Himself was not divisive and He never defended Himself. As His followers, people may stumble or be offended at the ways God leads us but if we truly entrust ourselves into His hands, then we have nothing to fear and no need to legitimize ourselves according to other people's measurements and ways of doing things. Paul's theology was based on one thing and one thing only—Jesus Christ and Him crucified—because anything beyond this is no longer the grace of God. There is no arguing in heaven, and heaven does not have a debate club. Even correction and rebukes can be given in love and in a way that builds believers up to new levels of freedom in the Lord rather than condemning them or tearing them down.

Jesus said that He had glorified God by finishing the work God had given Him to do. (see John 17:4) Similarly, towards the end of Paul's life, he knew that he had completed his God-given assignment and was ready to leave this world to be with the Lord. (see 2 Timothy 4:7) While we are here on earth, it is our job to get into alignment with God's will for us in order that we, too, may fulfill His purpose for us as we co-labor with Him.

> *2 Timothy 4:5 - But you, keep your head in all situations, endure hardship, do the work of an evangelist, discharge all the duties of your ministry.*

> *Colossians 4:17 - Tell Archippus: "See to it that you complete the ministry you have received in the Lord."*

LABORERS IN THE FIELD

When Paul moved into new territories or amongst unbelievers who had not yet heard the Good News of Jesus Christ the Messiah of Israel, he asked fellow believers to pray for him. These were Paul's prayer requests:

> *Colossians 4:3-4 KJV - Withal praying also for us, that God would open unto us a door of utterance, to speak the mystery of Christ, for which I am also in bonds: That I may make it manifest, as I ought to speak.*

> *Ephesians 6:19-20 - Pray also for me, that whenever I speak, words may be given me so that I will fearlessly make known the mystery of the gospel, for which I am an ambassador in chains. Pray that I may declare it fearlessly, as I should.*

Paul asked for God to *open a door of utterance,* which means to grant him opportunities to share the Gospel without hindrance. Opposition to the Gospel is to be expected as normal. Persecution and riotous attacks from Jews and Gentiles who reject our message of Jesus as their Messiah, Lord, and King, are exactly what Jesus told us we would encounter as His co-laborers. (see John 15:18-16:2) We must walk by the guidance of the Holy Spirit in order to know where God wants us to be and with whom He wants us to share the Gospel. However, even when we have a clear indication from the Holy Spirit that we are supposed to be somewhere in order to share the Lord with them, it can seem as if every possible deterrent to our being there begins to emerge. Only God can make a way for any of us to be where He wants us to be in His timing, and only He is able to open a door for powerful and effective work in the midst of great opposition. (see 1 Corinthians 16:9) We can effortlessly walk through the doors God opens for us if we remain faithful to His leading, do not allow ourselves to become discouraged by obstacles, wait for His timing, and move forward fearlessly when He gives us the go ahead.

Paul also asked for God to supply him with supernatural boldness. Opposition from the world, the flesh, and the devil functions through the words and actions of other people but also through the internal battles in our own minds. The world tries to convince us that its ways and rewards are superior to God's. Our flesh and pride prefer instant gratification and exaltation to the sacrificial living required of a servant of the Lord and we may endure massive and prolonged rejection before breakthrough comes in any given territory or people group. The devil attacks us with lies, accusations, and persecutions against God's will and our ability to carry it out. As God's co-laborers in the field of the unsaved, we need strength from God to push through all of this external and internal resistance in order to do God's work. This comes only when we know God's love deep within our soul so that we ourselves are fully persuaded of the message that we are sharing and the need to share it. Then, our fearlessness becomes a demonstration of our faith in God's goodness and our love becomes an appealing invitation into His family. On this note, we cannot confuse brashness with boldness. Praying for supernatural boldness as a servant of the Lord means being empowered with confidence to be kind and gracious in a world full of hate and animosity. We are sent with Good News as ambassadors of God's great love for all people, not with bad news of judgment and condemnation. There is nothing supernatural about obnoxiousness.

Additionally, Paul asked that God would give him the ability to present the Good News in a way that would make it plain and clear to those who heard it. God worked such a marvelous masterpiece of redemption in the death, resurrection, and ascension of His Son that it can be challenging, especially for an expert in the Scriptures, to describe it without becoming overly complex or confusing. However, we should be able to share the Gospel in a way that even a child can understand it and in a way that exalts God's work and not our own intellectual capabilities or powers of persuasion. In fact, Paul's approach to sharing the Gospel was so straightforward that false apostles ridiculed his non-argumentative, non-intellectual style of presentation. In Paul's own words, this is how he describes the mystery of the Gospel:

> *Ephesians 3:6 - This mystery is that through the gospel the Gentiles are heirs together with Israel, members together of one body, and sharers together in the promise in Christ Jesus.*

> *1 Timothy 3:16 - Beyond all question, the mystery from which true godliness springs is great: He appeared in the flesh, was vindicated by the Spirit, was seen by angels, was preached among the nations, was believed on in the world, was taken up in glory.*

> *Colossians 1:27-28 - To them God has chosen to make known among the Gentiles the glorious riches of this mystery, which is Christ in you, the hope of glory. He is the one we proclaim, admonishing and teaching everyone with all wisdom, so that we may present everyone fully mature in Christ.*

In addition to making the Gospel clear through his words, Paul made the Gospel clear through his actions and through manifestations of God's power. The Gospel is the power of God, and the power of God is the Gospel. (see Romans 1:16-17) Where the true Gospel is proclaimed, God backs it with miracles, signs, and wonders. Where God works miracles, signs, and wonders through one of His servants, He opens an opportunity to share the word of Christ and give credit to the One who is truly working the miracles. When the mystery of the Gospel seems too bizarre to understand mentally, manifestations of God's power breaks through intellectual barriers. Though the world offers counterfeits and religion attempts to disprove or discredit the miraculous, nobody can argue with someone who knows that *I was blind and now I see, and it happened because of Jesus.*

Paul also asked believers to pray that God would multiply his labors through the genuine faith and transformed lives of the new believers in every territory where God sent him. These were Paul's prayer requests for himself and praises for the believers:

> *2 Thessalonians 3:1 - As for other matters, brothers and sisters, pray for us that the message of the Lord may spread rapidly and be honored, just as it was with you.*

> *Romans 1:8 - First, I thank my God through Jesus Christ for all of you, because your faith is being reported all over the world.*

> *Romans 16:19 - Everyone has heard about your obedience, so I rejoice because of you; but I want you to be wise about what is good, and innocent about what is evil.*

In particular, the Thessalonians and the Romans received the Good News of Christ so deeply in their hearts that in the midst of persecution against them as followers of Christ, the genuineness of their faith became the talk of the world. In a day without television, radio, or internet, reports of their faith traveled near and far and, in effect, the news carried with it the message of the Gospel.

> *1 Thessalonians 1:8-10 - The Lord's message rang out from you not only in Macedonia and Achaia--your faith in God has become known everywhere. Therefore we do not need to say anything about it, for they themselves report what kind of reception you gave us. They tell how you turned to God from idols to serve the living and true God, and to wait for his Son from heaven, whom he raised from the dead--Jesus, who rescues us from the coming wrath.*

As God's co-laborers, we do our best to make the Gospel clear and reveal Jesus as He really is, but only God can truly work it into someone's heart. We desire for our impact to be as deep as possible when we are with people, but once we leave them we leave them in God's hands and what they truly believe will be revealed in due time. Jesus often sent people back to their family and village to tell about what the Lord had done for them, and our work as His co-laborers can be multiplied in this same way. When this happens, even a newborn disciple proclaims the Gospel without words and reveals the power of God through their transformed life. Genuine change becomes evident to their family, friends, acquaintances, and co-workers until it eventually impacts their city, nation, and the world. Paul prayed that, by the grace of God, this would happen among the new believers so that he could continue to focus on proclaiming the Gospel in new territories.

> *2 Corinthians 10:15-16 - Neither do we go beyond our limits by boasting of work done by others. Our hope is that, as your faith continues to grow, our sphere of activity among you will greatly expand, so that we can preach the gospel in the regions beyond you. For we do not want to boast about work already done in someone else's territory.*

Some of us are called by God to reveal the Gospel to unbelievers locally, and some of us are called by God to proclaim the Gospel where it has never been preached. Both are necessary for the fulfillment of Jesus' command to us as His disciples to make disciples from all nations. May our work as God's co-laborers among the unsaved be well received and multiplied until the Gospel is proclaimed to the whole world!

LABORERS IN THE CHURCH

Paul prayed and asked believers to pray for his labors within the Body of Christ among those who were growing as disciples of Jesus. God's purpose through the Gospel does not end with a one-time hearing of and believing in Jesus. The Gospel continues into every aspect of a believer's life until we are fully transformed into children of God who love like Jesus loved and are united with one another in our common faith. These were Paul's prayers and prayer requests:

1 Thessalonians 3:10 - Night and day we pray most earnestly that we may see you again and supply what is lacking in your faith.

Romans 1:9-12 - God, whom I serve in my spirit in preaching the gospel of his Son, is my witness how constantly I remember you in my prayers at all times; and I pray that now at last by God's will the way may be opened for me to come to you. I long to see you so that I may impart to you some spiritual gift to make you strong-- that is, that you and I may be mutually encouraged by each other's faith.

Romans 15:32 - [Pray] that I may come to you with joy, by God's will, and in your company be refreshed.

Philemon 1:6-7 - I pray that your partnership with us in the faith may be effective in deepening your understanding of every good thing we share for the sake of Christ. Your love has given me great joy and encouragement, because you, brother, have refreshed the hearts of the Lord's people.

Paul prayed that God would make a way for Him to visit believers in person whom he had not yet met and to re-visit believers whom he had previously met. Face-to-face meetings are essential for us to stay encouraged, grow to maturity, and draw together in unity with one another as the Body of Christ. In our modern world, although much can be accomplished through anointed writings, recordings, or videos, there will never be any comparison to in-person meetings of believers where the palpable and manifest presence of the Lord is experienced. When an anointed servant of the Lord leads His disciples in corporate worship, waiting upon Him, and following His lead, an atmosphere of Heaven takes over our meetings. The Holy Spirit honors God's servants by distributing spiritual gifts to strengthen, encourage, comfort, and heal one another so that we depart from our time together equipped and ready to combat the forces of darkness until we meet again. (see 1 Corinthians 12) A truly anointed servant of the Lord will help all believers to be refreshed in faith, refilled with the Holy Spirit, strengthened in love for one another, and to grow deeper in understanding God's goodness.

91

Paul also prayed to visit believers so they could encourage him. Leaders and full-time servants in the Kingdom of God encounter intense and daily opposition from people and from the evil one, which can make it challenging to stay encouraged. Moreover, true servants of the Lord are not working for the praise or approval of other people and often do not receive any recognition at all. As we learned in the last chapter, Paul was most encouraged to hear of believers' growing love and deepening faith because it revealed that his labor for the Lord had succeeded in planting a genuine seed of Christ in their hearts. Testimonies of God's goodness and miracles encourage us to remain heavenly-minded and hopeful. Stories of endurance through hardship and suffering for the name of Jesus remind us of the battle to which we have been called and strengthen our resolve to remain faithful to the one true God. Those of us who have given way to complacency need some Godly motivation and provocation to good works. Those who are discouraged need a boost of strength-giving joy in the Lord. Those who are too weak to press on by themselves need a helping hand. (see 1 Thessalonians 5:14)

In fact, Paul emphasized the immense value of believers supporting and praying for one another. In his travels, Paul gathered an offering from the churches to bring back to Jerusalem for the believers in Judea who were suffering from famine. Disciples of Christ in other parts of the world who had abundance were able to give generously so that the Judean Christians were well supplied in the midst of their hardship. As he collected the offering, Paul made it clear that the monetary value of gifts given to these fellow brothers and sisters in the faith was of equal or lesser value than the praises to God that would result from their gift and the prayers that the Judean believers would pray for them as their only way of saying thank you.

> *2 Corinthians 9:11-15 - You will be enriched in every way so that you can be generous on every occasion, and through us your generosity will result in thanksgiving to God. This service that you perform is not only supplying the needs of the Lord's people but is also overflowing in many expressions of thanks to God. Because of the service by which you have proved yourselves, others will praise God for the obedience that accompanies your*

confession of the gospel of Christ, and for your generosity in sharing with them and with everyone else. And in their prayers for you their hearts will go out to you, because of the surpassing grace God has given you. Thanks be to God for his indescribable gift!

Paul valued the prayers of other believers so much that when he could not be with the churches in person, he sent letters to them (even from prison) and sent messengers to ensure that the churches were well informed of his victories, struggles, persecutions, and the status of his imprisonment. (see Colossians 4:7-9; Ephesians 6:21-22) He did this so they would be encouraged by the example of his faith and so they could pray for him and support him in his labors and sufferings for the Lord. We are in this together, and praying for one another is essential to our perseverance and growth in the Lord to full unity and maturity in Him.

Ephesians 6:18 - And pray in the Spirit on all occasions with all kinds of prayers and requests. With this in mind, be alert and always keep on praying for all the Lord's people.

Colossians 4:12 - Epaphras, who is one of you and a servant of Christ Jesus, sends greetings. He is always wrestling in prayer for you, that you may stand firm in all the will of God, mature and fully assured.

Throughout his letters, Paul particularly honored leaders in the churches. He praised by name those who opened their homes in order for believers to worship with one another, those who had received and refreshed him in his travels, and those who faithfully served the Lord with genuine love. He urged believers to do everything possible to support God's appointed leaders, love them, submit to them, and see to it they had everything that was needed for the fulfillment of God's purposes.

1 Thessalonians 5:12-13 - Now we ask you, brothers and sisters, to acknowledge those who work hard among you, who care for you in the Lord and who admonish you. Hold them in the highest regard in love because of their work. Live in peace with each other.

Not everyone receives a public thank you from the Apostle Paul that makes it into the Bible. However, though it may seem like a small thing, sometimes a simple acknowledgement, encouragement, or small contribution to a true laborer's work can bring great joy. Also, settling disputes without requiring the leader's assistance whenever possible also helps leaders to stay free to focus on the Lord and deeper spiritual needs of the community.

As sons and daughters of God, we are family. We need one another. We can never forget that it is the way that we take care of one another that reveals the love of Jesus to the world. Fellow believers, full-time laborers, and God's appointed leaders deserve highest priority when it comes to our prayers and support. As we pray for all believers, we become poignantly aware that we are part of something much greater than ourselves and we have the privilege of watching the hand of God move on behalf of His children all over the world.

TRAVEL

Paul's prayers and prayer requests for himself also included praying for his travels. We have already discussed God's exclusive ability to open doors for His servants, and Paul knew very well that he would only be able to be somewhere if the Lord made a way for him. These were Paul's prayers and prayer requests for travel:

> *Philemon 1:22 - And one thing more: Prepare a guest room for me, because I hope to be restored to you in answer to your prayers. (written from prison)*

> *1 Thessalonians 3:10-11 - Night and day we pray most earnestly that we may see you again and supply what is lacking in your faith. Now may our God and Father himself and our Lord Jesus clear the way for us to come to you.*

> *Romans 1:9-13 - God, whom I serve in my spirit in preaching the gospel of his Son, is my witness how constantly I remember you in my prayers at all times; and I pray that now at last by God's will the way may be opened for me to come to you. I long to see you so that I may impart to you some spiritual gift to make you strong-- that is, that you and I may be mutually encouraged by each other's faith. I do not want you to be unaware, brothers and*

sisters, that I planned many times to come to you (but have been prevented from doing so until now) in order that I might have a harvest among you, just as I have had among the other Gentiles.

Romans 15:32 - [Pray] that I may come to you with joy, by God's will, and in your company be refreshed.

Colossians 4:3 - And pray for us, too, that God may open a door for our message, so that we may proclaim the mystery of Christ, for which I am in chains.

Paul was guided by the Lord in all of His travels. (see Acts 13-28) In fact, his entire life in the Lord was based on obedience to the vision of the Lord and His command to turn all people from darkness to light and from the power of satan to God. When Paul first came to faith in Jesus, the Holy Spirit led him into the wilderness of Arabia for three years. Many years later, it was the Holy Spirit who set him apart with Barnabas and sent him on his first missionary journey from Antioch. The Holy Spirit prevented him from going to Asia and Bithynia until he had a vision of a Macedonian man, which set his course for Philippi. The evil one blocked his ability to get to the Thessalonian believers, but the Lord appeared to Paul in a vision and told him to remain in Corinth and continue proclaiming the Gospel. When it was time for him to depart, Paul promised the Corinthian believers that he would return to them only if it was the Lord's will. Soon, he began to know that it was God's will for him to go to Rome, but despite his plans to go to there, God did not make a way for him to be there yet. Instead, he was compelled by the Holy Spirit to visit a few churches on his way to Jerusalem and felt bound by the Holy Spirit to go there regardless of the fact that believers everywhere were telling him not to go to Jerusalem because they knew prophetically that he would face suffering and imprisonment. During his imprisonment in Jerusalem, the Lord appeared to Paul to encourage him and reassure him that he was indeed on his way to Rome to preach the Gospel. He traveled to Rome as a prisoner on trial who had appealed to Caesar for justice and, even then, an angel appeared to Paul to tell him that their ship would be wrecked but all the passengers would survive on account of God's love and purpose for him. He made it to Rome and faithfully proclaimed the Gospel, even while under house arrest.

Needless to say, God's travel plans for us and our ways of thinking do not always line up, but God has His ways of getting us exactly where He wants us to be. This makes it all the more important that we pray to stay in step with the Lord and His purposes rather than our own agenda and desires. God can easily get us anywhere and He can also block us from being where He does not want us to be. Both are for our good. As God guides our paths, we are strengthened by the Holy Spirit even if the Lord leads us into suffering for His name. We can press through the enemy's attempts to stop us from being where God wants us to be, and we can be confident in God's protection when He exercises veto power to cancel our plans. For this reason, when Paul spoke of his own travel or requested that his co-laborers come to visit him, he always said, "Lord willing," and "Do your best."

DELIVERANCE FROM PERSECUTORS

Paul encountered incredible opposition to his work from religious Jews who denied Jesus as their Messiah, from unbelieving Gentiles who preferred the ways of darkness, and from false teachers who relentlessly attacked his ministry at every turn. He suffered for the name of the Lord Jesus with honor and with rejoicing because he knew that all of his sufferings worked out for the benefit of the Church and the glory of God.

> *2 Corinthians 6:3-10 - We put no stumbling block in anyone's path, so that our ministry will not be discredited. Rather, as servants of God we commend ourselves in every way: in great endurance; in troubles, hardships and distresses; in beatings, imprisonments and riots; in hard work, sleepless nights and hunger; in purity, understanding, patience and kindness; in the Holy Spirit and in sincere love; in truthful speech and in the power of God; with weapons of righteousness in the right hand and in the left; through glory and dishonor, bad report and good report; genuine, yet regarded as impostors; known, yet regarded as unknown; dying, and yet we live on; beaten, and yet not killed; sorrowful, yet always rejoicing; poor, yet making many rich; having nothing, and yet possessing everything.*

> *2 Corinthians 11:23-27 - Are they servants of Christ? (I am out of*

my mind to talk like this.) I am more. I have worked much harder, been in prison more frequently, been flogged more severely, and been exposed to death again and again. Five times I received from the Jews the forty lashes minus one. Three times I was beaten with rods, once I was pelted with stones, three times I was shipwrecked, I spent a night and a day in the open sea, I have been constantly on the move. I have been in danger from rivers, in danger from bandits, in danger from my fellow Jews, in danger from Gentiles; in danger in the city, in danger in the country, in danger at sea; and in danger from false believers. I have labored and toiled and have often gone without sleep; I have known hunger and thirst and have often gone without food; I have been cold and naked.

Colossians 1:24 - Now I rejoice in what I am suffering for you, and I fill up in my flesh what is still lacking in regard to Christ's afflictions, for the sake of his body, which is the church.

Paul rejoiced in his afflictions because he knew that everywhere he went, everyone knew that he was there because he was a servant of the Lord Jesus Christ. In one instance, the hand of God released Paul from his prison shackles by the power of a great earthquake and, because of this, the prison guard and his whole household came to faith. Paul learned to rely on God even in the face of death and acknowledged that the prayers of the saints for him played an important role in his victorious deliverance.

2 Corinthians 1:8-11 - We do not want you to be uninformed, brothers and sisters, about the troubles we experienced in the province of Asia. We were under great pressure, far beyond our ability to endure, so that we despaired of life itself. Indeed, we felt we had received the sentence of death. But this happened that we might not rely on ourselves but on God, who raises the dead. He has delivered us from such a deadly peril, and he will deliver us again. On him we have set our hope that he will continue to deliver us, as you help us by your prayers. Then many will give thanks on our behalf for the gracious favor granted us in answer to the prayers of many.

Philippians 1:19 - for I know that through your prayers and God's provision of the Spirit of Jesus Christ what has happened to me will turn out for my deliverance. (written from prison)

In fact, in the midst of fatigue and despair, Paul relied upon the prayers of fellow believers for protection from wicked opponents to the work of the Lord. These were Paul's prayer requests for himself:

2 Thessalonians 3:2-3 - And pray that we may be delivered from wicked and evil people, for not everyone has faith. But the Lord is faithful, and he will strengthen you and protect you from the evil one.

Romans 15:30-32 - I urge you, brothers and sisters, by our Lord Jesus Christ and by the love of the Spirit, to join me in my struggle by praying to God for me. Pray that I may be kept safe from the unbelievers in Judea and that the contribution I take to Jerusalem may be favorably received by the Lord's people there, so that I may come to you with joy, by God's will, and in your company be refreshed.

Interestingly, Paul did not pray for every unbeliever that crossed his path to come to faith in Jesus. Though it was his sincere desire for everyone to come to faith, it was more significant to him to stay in step with God's purpose and assignment for him, even if that meant dodging certain people or being miraculously released from their grip. Jesus died for all people but not everyone accepts the free gift of eternal life. Often, those who reject the message of God's love aggressively attack the message and also its messengers. From these people, we need God's protection. Interestingly, there was only one occasion when Paul cast a demon out of someone who did not come to him in faith asking for help. A Philippian slave girl with a spirit of divination was a full-time fortune-teller for profit. She followed Paul around, announcing accurately that Paul was a servant of the Most High God. Regardless of the fact that she was speaking the truth, everything else about her work was not of the Holy Spirit but was motivated by the demonic spirit and profit-seeking. Therefore, after many days of allowing this to continue, Paul finally felt the need to put an end to it by casting the demon out of her so that unbelievers and new believers would not confuse his work and hers. (see Acts 16:16-18) All of this is to say that Paul did not waste time forcing conversion on opponents or using his authority against people's will. His only desire was to be unhindered by opponents so that he could reach those who would believe in the message of Christ and be saved.

On the other hand, Paul did not always pray to be delivered. At one point in his life, he would rather have died and been with the Lord, but he knew that it was necessary for him to live so that he could continue his Kingdom labor on earth for Him. But, by the time his martyrdom drew near, he knew it. He accepted the will of the Lord with joy. He knew that his time on earth was completed and the Lord had eternal rewards for him in heaven. He had learned to be content in all circumstances because the Lord gave him strength no matter what. (see Philippians 4:11-13)

> *2 Timothy 4:7-8, 16-18 - I have fought the good fight, I have finished the race, I have kept the faith. Now there is in store for me the crown of righteousness, which the Lord, the righteous Judge, will award to me on that day--and not only to me, but also to all who have longed for his appearing. ... At my first defense, no one came to my support, but everyone deserted me. May it not be held against them. But the Lord stood at my side and gave me strength, so that through me the message might be fully proclaimed and all the Gentiles might hear it. And I was delivered from the lion's mouth. The Lord will rescue me from every evil attack and will bring me safely to his heavenly kingdom. To him be glory for ever and ever. Amen.*

As we set out to do the work of the Lord for our lives, we can be certain that we will face opposition, persecution, and resistance from unbelievers, believers, and from the evil one. Sometimes God will move in miraculous ways to deliver us, and other times we will suffer at the hands of cruel and wicked people for the name of Jesus. In all of this, we can rejoice knowing that our eternal rewards are much greater than anything this world has to offer us. We must persist in prayer for one another to stay in step with the Lord and rejoice in Him whether He leads us into peace or persecution, whether He delivers us to more co-laboring or calls us home to heaven.

FALSE LABORERS

As Paul encountered resistance to his work of spreading the Gospel, he took note of false laborers who attacked him and used the name of Jesus in error. He warned believers in the churches to watch out for false teachers and to stay on guard in their beliefs and simple devotion. These are some of the things Paul had to say about false laborers:

1 Timothy 1:20 - Among them are Hymenaeus and Alexander, whom I have handed over to Satan to be taught not to blaspheme.

2 Timothy 2:16-18 - Avoid godless chatter, because those who indulge in it will become more and more ungodly. Their teaching will spread like gangrene. Among them are Hymenaeus and Philetus, who have departed from the truth. They say that the resurrection has already taken place, and they destroy the faith of some.

2 Timothy 4:14-15 - Alexander the metalworker did me a great deal of harm. The Lord will repay him for what he has done. You too should be on your guard against him, because he strongly opposed our message.

Act 20:28-31 - Keep watch over yourselves and all the flock of which the Holy Spirit has made you overseers. Be shepherds of the church of God, which he bought with his own blood. I know that after I leave, savage wolves will come in among you and will not spare the flock. Even from your own number men will arise and distort the truth in order to draw away disciples after them. So be on your guard! Remember that for three years I never stopped warning each of you night and day with tears.

Galatians 1:8-9 - But even if we or an angel from heaven should preach a gospel other than the one we preached to you, let them be under God's curse! As we have already said, so now I say again: If anybody is preaching to you a gospel other than what you accepted, let them be under God's curse!

1 Timothy 6:3-5 - If anyone teaches otherwise and does not agree to the sound instruction of our Lord Jesus Christ and to godly teaching, they are conceited and understand nothing. They have an unhealthy interest in controversies and quarrels about words that result in envy, strife, malicious talk, evil suspicions and constant friction between people of corrupt mind, who have been robbed of the truth and who think that godliness is a means to financial gain.

Paul certainly used strong and emphatic language for false laborers who took advantage of vulnerable believers by preaching the Gospel for personal gain or who perverted the simplicity of the Gospel in order to make a name for themselves. However, in only one instance did Paul use his authority to demonstrate the superiority of Christ to a false laborer who was hindering the potential faith of a new believer. The governor of Paphos desired to hear the Gospel, but a Jewish sorcerer who was employed as his spiritual advisor did everything he could to prevent Paul from sharing the news of Christ with him. Paul rightfully named the false sorcerer as an enemy of everything good and cursed him with temporary blindness. Seeing this, the governor definitively believed Jesus. (see Acts 13:6-12)

Aside from this instance, Paul did not waste time or abuse his authority by cursing false teachers, but instead kept himself focused on doing the work of the Lord in spite of their attempts to hinder him. For example, when fellow believers were unsupportive of Paul's ministry and even when they abandoned him to the hands of his persecutors, he did not hold it against them. More than this, he exhorted that opponents be shown patience and mercy in love and hope that their faith may be purified.

2 Timothy 4:16 - At my first defense, no one came to my support, but everyone deserted me. May it not be held against them.

2 Timothy 2:25-26 - Opponents must be gently instructed, in the hope that God will grant them repentance leading them to a knowledge of the truth, and that they will come to their senses and escape from the trap of the devil, who has taken them captive to do his will.

This is significant because it is not always easy to discern false teachers from real ones. As a matter of fact, as Paul proclaimed the Gospel of Jesus Christ, he was more accused than anyone else of being a false laborer for the Lord. False accusation is the devil's favorite tactic for stirring up suspicion, division, religion, and the same spirit that crucified Jesus. This means that we must be careful about becoming overly skeptical, paranoid, and prejudiced against those who worship Jesus a little differently than we do.

Jesus instructed His disciples not to stop those who were working miracles in His name just because they were not part of their particular group, and Paul rejoiced that the Gospel was proclaimed even if it was by those who were selfishly motivated. (see Mark 9:38-41; Philippians 1:15-18) Those who are not against Jesus are for Him, and we can trust God to work out the finer points. Though it can be more obvious to point out wrong practices of saying that evil things are good, it is equally offensive to God when we fail to discern a good thing and call it evil. So, we must be cautious, discern with right judgment, and leave most things in the hands of the Lord alone. (see Isaiah 5:20; John 7:24) Jesus strongly rebuked His disciples for desiring to call fire down from heaven on those who were unwelcoming and pointed out that they were functioning in a wrong spirit. (see Luke 9:55)

Let us never forget that it was the set apart people of God, the very ones who should have recognized Jesus as their Messiah, who rejected Jesus as a false prophet, accused Jesus of working for the devil, and who sentenced Jesus to death as a blasphemer against God. This is the One that we follow, and He said that we could expect to be treated the same way. In fact, if we have not yet been accused of being a false laborer, then we're probably not much of a real one. The evil one attacks one real servant of the Lord more ruthlessly and with more unwavering persistence than a thousand half-hearted disciples combined. Unfortunately, he often uses professing believers to carry out many of his accusations and attacks. Therefore, we should stay on guard from false laborers, but we must also be careful that we do not establish ourselves in our own doctrines and traditions so much that we accidentally guard ourselves from God and

His true servants.

Granted, Jesus told His followers to beware of allowing the teachings of the religious leaders and the ways of the world to pollute our faith. However, He died for the sins of all mankind, even those who opposed Him, crying out with His final breath, "Forgive them, Father, for they know not what they do." (see Luke 23:34) Remember that Paul had once been a zealous religious teacher who contradicted and opposed the Gospel with every fiber of his being until he had an encounter with the Lord that changed his life forever. The Lord showed Paul mercy because he had acted in ignorance and unbelief. This means that there is hope for anyone and that until Jesus returns, even false teachers have time to repent.

OUR JOB DESCRIPTION

Every single follower of Jesus has been commissioned by the Lord for a purpose. God's eternal redemptive plan is His assignment for us even though the way that we serve God in our various ministries may be different. No matter what forms of service the Lord has called us to, all of us have the same job description.

> *Mathew 28:19-20 - "Therefore go and make disciples of all nations, baptizing them in the name of the Father and of the Son and of the Holy Spirit, and teaching them to obey everything I have commanded you. And surely I am with you always, to the very end of the age."*

> *2 Corinthians 5:18-19 - All this is from God, who reconciled us to himself through Christ and gave us the ministry of reconciliation: that God was reconciling the world to himself in Christ, not counting people's sins against them. And he has committed to us the message of reconciliation.*

> *Ephesians 4:11-13 - So Christ himself gave the apostles, the prophets, the evangelists, the pastors and teachers, to equip his people for works of service, so that the body of Christ may be built up until we all reach unity in the faith and in the knowledge of the Son of God and become mature, attaining to the whole measure of the fullness of Christ.*

2 Timothy 2:15 - Do your best to present yourself to God as one approved, a worker who does not need to be ashamed and who correctly handles the word of truth.

John 13:34-35 - "A new command I give you: Love one another. As I have loved you, so you must love one another. By this everyone will know that you are my disciples, if you love one another."

Our job as God's co-laborers is clear. Go into all nations to make disciples by showing them the way to have peace with God. Each of us is called to equip the Church for ministry and for unity and maturity, stay grounded in the truth of the Word of God, live lives worthy of His calling, and love one another as Jesus loves us.

In one of Jesus' parables about laborers, He expressed how we have been given certain resources that were given to us by God for the purpose of building His Kingdom. Those of us who know that God is good and invest all that we have been given into His eternal plan will be greatly rewarded by Him. But those who give way to lukewarm complacency or use what they have been given by God for their own purposes simply demonstrate that they do not understand God's heart. (see Matthew 25:14-30; Luke 19:11-26) In another parable, Jesus made clear that while we are laboring with God and with one another, there is no room for competition or accusations against God about unfairness toward us. We are all laboring in the same field, for the same purpose, and for one Master who will fairly divide the spoils at the end of the day. (see Matthew 20:1-16)

Until then, may each one of us be led by the Holy Spirit to put our hand to the plow in God's harvest fields and not look back. (see Luke 9:62) May we fulfill the ministries God has given us as we co-labor with Him for His Kingdom. Amen.

CHAPTER SIX

FOR ISRAEL AND
THE NATIONS
(THE LOST)

BE WISE IN THE WAY YOU ACT TOWARD OUTSIDERS;
MAKE THE MOST OF EVERY OPPORTUNITY. LET
YOUR CONVERSATION BE ALWAYS FULL OF GRACE,
SEASONED WITH SALT, SO THAT YOU MAY KNOW
HOW TO ANSWER EVERYONE.
– THE APOSTLE PAUL, COLOSSIANS 4:5-6

It has always been God's desire for all people to come to faith in Him and to know Him. This said, the Apostle Paul did not give us an example of praying for the lost. Instead, he gave his life to proclaiming the Gospel so that everyone could hear the Good News of Jesus Christ and be saved. Jesus did not pray for the lost. He loved the world so much that He gave His life for them. Now He sends us to go and do likewise so that the world might come to know His love.

> *John 17:9, 18, 20 – [Jesus praying] "I pray for them. I am not praying for the world, but for those you have given me, for they are yours. ... As you sent me into the world, I have sent them into the world. ... "My prayer is not for them alone. I pray also for those who will believe in me through their message,"*

Interestingly, this is consistent with the Biblical pattern for prayer. Abraham, at the impending destruction of Sodom and Gomorrah, appealed to God's perfectly just nature and said that it would be unfair of God if the righteous and the wicked received the same punishment just because they were in the same cities. He prayed for the righteous and for the cities to be spared on account of the righteous. In response to Abraham's prayer, and as a foreshadowing of the Day of Judgment to come, God destroyed the wicked cities and their inhabitants but rescued the righteous from destruction. (see Genesis 18:16-19:29) Later in history, when the people of Israel went astray and deserved God's wrath, Moses offered his own life in their place so that they could live. Moses pleaded with the Lord to have mercy on His people, reminding God that they were His special possession and asking God to remember His promises to the patriarchs rather than looking at Israel's recent failures. Moses also pointed out that if God destroyed His people in the wilderness, then the nations of the world would have good reason to doubt the God of Israel's good nature, ability to keep His promises, and superiority above the gods of all other nations. (see Exodus 32:11-13, 32; Deuteronomy 9:25-29) Daniel, Nehemiah, and Ezra also prayed for the covenant people of God by calling upon the Lord to remember His own nature of mercy and loving-kindness toward them as His people in spite of their sins and in order for God's own reputation in the sight of all the nations to be preserved and honored. (see Daniel 9:3-19; Nehemiah 9:5-37; Ezra 9:5-15)

God's Old Covenant design for Israel was not for them to be an evangelistic nation, reaching out to the whole world, but for them to be a shining light so the whole world would be able to recognize the superiority of Israel's God by the righteous way that they did things and the way that He blessed them. (see Deuteronomy 4:5-8, 28:10; Psalm 67) When Solomon dedicated the Temple of God in Jerusalem, he asked God to honor the prayers of foreigners and people from all nations who came to worship Him as the one true God. God's house was always intended to be a house of prayer for people from all nations to come and pray to Him. (see 1 Kings 8:41-43; Isaiah 56:7) Incidentally, in Jesus' day, the only area in the Temple which gave foreigners a place to worship the God of Israel had been turned into a marketplace, set up to take advantage of people rather than welcome those who did not know God. The religious leaders had strayed far from God's purpose for His people and this is one of the primary reasons why Jesus so passionately cleared out their merchandising activities. (see Matthew 21:12-13)

When Nineveh, a Gentile city, was deserving of judgment, God did not instruct His people to pray from a distance for the people of Nineveh. Instead, He sent Jonah, a prophet of Israel, to bring a message to them that they needed to change their ways or be met with God's wrath. Similarly, God did not keep His distance and intercede from heaven for the whole world. He sent Jesus, His one and only Son, as a walking, talking, vessel of His mercy and grace so that all who believe in Him can know God and escape the wrath to come at the end of the age. After Jesus' resurrection from the grave, He did not command His followers to pray for the lost but commissioned His disciples to go into all nations and demonstrate His love to the world. (see Matthew 28:19-20) Finally, in the Book of Acts, when persecution raged against the earliest Christian believers, the first of God's New Covenant people, they did not pray for unbelievers but instead, prayed for God to send them out into all the nations and to give them more boldness to proclaim the Gospel fearlessly.

> *Acts 4:24-30 - When they heard this, they raised their voices together in prayer to God. "Sovereign Lord," they said, "you made the heavens and the earth and the sea, and everything in them. You spoke by the Holy Spirit through the mouth of your servant, our father David: "'Why do the nations rage and the peoples plot in vain? The kings of the earth rise up and the rulers band together against the Lord and against his anointed one.' Indeed Herod and Pontius Pilate met together with the Gentiles and the people of Israel in this city to conspire against your holy servant Jesus, whom you anointed. They did what your power and will had decided beforehand should happen. Now, Lord, consider their threats and enable your servants to speak your word with great boldness. Stretch out your hand to heal and perform signs and wonders through the name of your holy servant Jesus."*

For the first several years of the Christian faith, as detailed in the Gospels and the first seven chapters of the Book of Acts, almost all of the earliest disciples were Jewish. In this prayer, they quoted the Second Psalm from the Scriptures. Psalm 2 is a Messianic Psalm, meaning that it speaks about the Messiah of Israel, the Son of God, who will conquer the world and rule the whole earth. In this Psalm, God the Father says to His Son, "Ask of me and I will give you the nations as your inheritance." (see Psalm 2:8) The word for *nations* here is the same word that Jews use to describe all non-Jews: *goim*. This word also means *heathen* or figuratively, *a group of wild animals.* To a certain extent, this is how Jews have regarded non-Jews because of the superiority of the God of Israel compared to the gods of all other people. These early believers took note that the nations or *goim* were raging against God's Messiah just as this Psalm had predicted. However, also in fulfillment of this Psalm, before His crucifixion, Jesus asked His Father to give Him all who would believe, both Jew and non-Jew, to be His people and His inheritance forever. (see John 17:20) Accordingly, and in line with God's heart for all people to be saved, the New Covenant includes salvation for people from all nations who come to faith in Jesus, even heathens who have raged against Him. (see Isaiah 42:9, 49:6; John 10:16) These earliest believers knew, as the Psalm says, that anyone who does not submit themselves to the Son of God will be destroyed. So, they asked for God to grant them supernatural power for telling everyone about Jesus. Then, after they finished praying, they went out into the world to do it. (see the rest of the Book of Acts)

All of this is to say that there is no Biblical example of prayer for the unsaved. Rather, there are many examples of God's "you first" policy towards His Old and New Covenant people. He reveals Himself to us so we can know Him and shows us His ways so we can be like Him and so His reputation in the earth is spread through our actions of love, mercy, righteousness, and blessing. We are the light of the world and our job as New Covenant believers is to tell unbelievers about Jesus' great love for them and also to love unbelievers so well that we leave them without excuse for not believing that Jesus is who He says He is. If we are hypocritical because our actions in our own lives do not match the words coming out of our mouths, then they have good reason not to trust the God we say we serve. If we are harsh, condemning, or unforgiving toward unbelievers, then we are not sharing the Good News with them at all. If we are self-righteous, judgmental, or hopeless in our thoughts toward the lost, then we only reveal that Christ has not been fully formed in us and that we do not fully understand the mercy and kindness He extended to us when we did not deserve it. Although none of us will die for the sins of others like Jesus did, as His followers we are called to take up our cross and die to ourselves so that His love is evident to those who desperately need to hear and experience the Good News of Christ.

This said, when people do not know the Lord, sometimes the things that they do can seem endlessly frustrating and take us to the edge of our patience. The best way to keep God's mercy at the forefront of our minds is to remember how lost, frustrating, and wearying we were before we knew Jesus. When we were clueless, arrogant, living a life of sin, or just plain chasing after the wind in vanity, Jesus reconciled us to the Father. (see Colossians 1:21-23) When we were God's enemy and powerless to help ourselves, Jesus died for us. (see Romans 5:6-10) More specifically, it is good to remember frequently what Jesus has done in our life, how He has changed us, and the things from which Jesus has healed, delivered, or rescued us. We must never forget the ways that Jesus has set us free from things that prevented us from being all that God designed us to be and the erroneous beliefs that Jesus has replaced with truth, love, and grace. And we must always keep in mind that, just like us, that lost person is dead in Christ's death and their sins have been judged at the cross just like ours have been. (see 2 Corinthians 5:14-19) Then, like Jesus who came not to judge but to save, we have genuine hearts as ambassadors of God's mercy. Our message is, "Repent for the Kingdom of Heaven is at hand!" which again, in effect, means, "Change your mind, believe that God loves you so much that He sent Jesus to die for your sins, and Heaven can be yours now." Of course, our message also includes, "I know it is true because He did it for me." This are some ways that Paul summarized it:

Acts 20:21 NLT - I have had one message for Jews and Greeks [Gentiles] alike--the necessity of repenting from sin and turning to God, and of having faith in our Lord Jesus.

Titus 2:11-15 - For the grace of God has appeared that offers salvation to all people. It teaches us to say "No" to ungodliness and worldly passions, and to live self-controlled, upright and godly lives in this present age, while we wait for the blessed hope-

-the appearing of the glory of our great God and Savior, Jesus Christ, who gave himself for us to redeem us from all wickedness and to purify for himself a people that are his very own, eager to do what is good. These, then, are the things you should teach. Encourage and rebuke with all authority. Do not let anyone despise you.

2 Timothy 2:19 - Nevertheless, God's solid foundation stands firm, sealed with this inscription: "The Lord knows those who are his," and, "Everyone who confesses the name of the Lord must turn away from wickedness." (quoting Numbers 16:5; Isaiah 52:11)

In every nation, tribe, and tongue, only God knows who are truly His. Since only God knows, our job is to make it available to everyone. Jesus died for all people, but not all people will respond to the Gospel and receive God's grace. Think of it this way. In the natural, real sheep know the voice of their shepherd and respond to it. If there was a pasture where the sheep of Shepherd A and Shepherd B are eating and drinking, when Shepherd A calls for his sheep to move on, Shepherd A's sheep will follow him. If Shepherd B calls out to Shepherd A's sheep, they will keep on eating and drinking because they do not follow the voice of another shepherd. Metaphorically speaking, every person in the world is a sheep, but only those who are Jesus' sheep will respond to His voice. Jesus never prayed for God to give His sheep ears to hear. Instead, He called out to everyone and was confident that those who had ears to hear would hear and obey His words of eternal life. He calls out in the same way today by using us as His delegates. Our job is to tell everyone in order to give them the opportunity to hear and believe. Those who are His will respond to His voice through our words as the Holy Spirit tells them about the love of God, changes their hearts, and shows them the way to eternal pasture.

When we pray for the lost, it can be beneficial for us to agree in prayer with what the Scriptures reveal to us regarding the different roles of the Father, Son, and Holy Spirit pertaining to the lost. We can ask God to draw the lost into Jesus. (see John 6:44) We can ask God or Jesus to send the Holy Spirit to testify to them about Jesus and to convict them of sin, righteousness, and judgment. (see John 15:26, 16:8) We can ask Jesus to have mercy on them, show compassion to them, intercede for them, and reveal the Father to them. (see John 14:6; Matthew 11:27) Additionally, as the Holy Spirit gives us faith to do so, we can pray the prayers that Paul prayed for believers—even for those who are not yet believers—and then leave the results in God's hands. But while we are praying for them, we must also love them so much and so selflessly that they wonder and ask why we are being so kind. Then we can tell them how kind Jesus has been to us.

FOR ISRAEL/THE JEWISH PEOPLE

The Jewish people have always been, and always will be, unlike every other nation in the whole wide world because they have a very special role in God's redemptive plan. The Apostle Paul had such a strong desire to see the Jewish people come to faith in Jesus as their Messiah that, like Moses and Jesus, he offered his own life in their place for the sake of their salvation and prayed ceaselessly to God that they might be saved. I do not believe that Paul's anguish for Israel was a result of personal patriotism due to his own Jewishness. Paul was a man who knew the Scriptures and understood God's heart, purposes, and plan for Israel.

> *Romans 9:3-5 - For I could wish that I myself were cursed and cut off from Christ for the sake of my people, those of my own race, the people of Israel. Theirs is the adoption to sonship; theirs the divine glory, the covenants, the receiving of the law, the temple worship and the promises. Theirs are the patriarchs, and from them is traced the human ancestry of the Messiah, who is God over all, forever praised! Amen.*

> *Romans 10:1 - Brothers and sisters, my heart's desire and prayer to God for the Israelites is that they may be saved.*

To put it plainly, Jesus is Jewish. Every book in the Bible was written by Jews, for Jews, about Jews, and to Jews. Jesus is the King of Israel. In point of fact, if Jesus is not the King of the Jews, then He is not the King of anything and He is certainly not the Savior of the world who crushes the serpent's head for the benefit of all mankind. (see Genesis 3:15) The Scriptures detail Jesus' genealogies in order to prove that He is the one and only Savior that the one and only God, who is the Creator of Heaven and earth, promised for the salvation of His people and for all mankind. Jesus was sent by God to make Himself known to all Israel and to seek, serve, and save the lost sheep of Israel. (see John 1:31; Matthew 10:6, 15:24) He died first and foremost for the Jewish people and also equally for non-Jews who would come to trust in Him as their Lord, Savior, and King.

> *John 11:51-52 - He [Caiaphas] did not say this on his own, but as high priest that year he prophesied that Jesus would die for the Jewish nation, and not only for that nation but also for the scattered children of God, to bring them together and make them one.*

Adhering to God's ultimate "you first" policy, Jesus offered salvation first to God's chosen people, the Jews. When Paul, the apostle to the Gentiles, proclaimed the Gospel in new territories, his practice was to find the local synagogue or meeting place of Jewish people in order to tell them first that God had sent their Messiah by sending Jesus in the flesh. Paul would not move on to preaching to Gentiles until the Jews had been given first right of refusal to hear the Gospel and either believe in Jesus or reject Him.

> *Romans 1:16 - For I am not ashamed of the gospel, because it is the power of God that brings salvation to everyone who believes: first to the Jew, then to the Gentile.*

While God does validly call for some of us as His children to bring the Gospel to a specific nation or people group, God does not stir everyone's heart for that nation. But, I submit to you that God calls every follower of Jesus to the Jewish people because of their unique place in His heart. Jews were chosen by God first, loved by God first, and will be judged by God first at the end of the age.

> *Romans 2:9-11 - There will be trouble and distress for every human being who does evil: first for the Jew, then for the Gentile; but glory, honor and peace for everyone who does good: first for the Jew, then for the Gentile. For God does not show favoritism.*

Therefore, they maintain their position as deserving the first right of refusal in hearing the message of the Gospel. This is unquestionably the

Biblical pattern presented in both the Old and New Testaments and expresses God's character and faithfulness in keeping His word.

Let me put it to you this way: Jews have been waiting for their promised Messiah for thousands of years. If you had been waiting thousands of years for something, wouldn't you want someone to make it a priority to tell you that it had arrived? Or, if you had entered into a contract with a business person which stated that you would be the recipient of their goods when the goods became available, would it be right for them to give those goods to someone else without honoring their agreement with you? Accordingly, if we truly believe in God's faithfulness in keeping His promises, then how could we think that He would abandon His people, the object of His affection, or be untrue to His covenant with them?

Along this same line of thinking, the New Covenant was given to the people of Israel who had the Old Covenant, which promised that there would be a New one. By name, there cannot, and would not, be a New Covenant unless there had been an Old one. The New Covenant was given first to the Jews and extends to share the blessings of God with non-Jews. (see Isaiah 42:6, 49:6) In fact, it was such a shock to the Jewish believers in Jesus for non-Jews to be included in the New Covenant that it took three visions from heaven and God sovereignly pouring out the Holy Spirit to Gentiles at Cornelius' house to affirm His will on the matter. (see Acts 10:1-11:18) The hot theological debate of the early Church, which consisted mostly of Jewish believers, was whether or not non-Jews had to be circumcised in their flesh in order to be considered part of God's people at all. (see Acts 15:1-29) How times have changed! Nonetheless, this means that, if like me, you were not Jewish at birth, then we should be eternally grateful to the Jews for the roots of our faith and ready to graciously share with them what Jesus has done for them!

God has not rejected the Jewish people and the Church has not replaced Israel. Paul clearly articulated that when he speaks of Israel, he speaks of those of his own race, meaning the Jewish people. (see Romans 9:6) There are seventy-two uses of "Israel" in the New Testament and not one of them refers to the Church, either literally or metaphorically. Believers in Rome became confused about this matter because they began to regard the expulsion of the Jews and harsh persecution against them as a sign that God had rejected them as His people as punishment for rejecting Jesus as their Messiah. However, Paul strongly rebuked them for this erroneous belief. He said, "God forbid" which is the Hebrew idiom, *"chas v'chalila."* This expression is used to indicate that a thought is sick, twisted, or beneath one's dignity or honor. (see Romans 3:4, 31, 6:2, 7:7, 13, 9:6, 14, 11:1, 11) God has not become anti-Semitic. His Son is still Jewish. It is a dangerous misunderstanding of God's character for us to think that He has in any way broken His word to His Old Covenant people or replaced them with another group of people. If He has been fickle in keeping His promises to them, then we should be very concerned that He might back out of His New Covenant assurances to us.

Granted, it is true that the Jews in Jesus' day rejected and crucified Him. And yet, this has not altered the special status of the Jewish people in God's sight. He loves them, not because of their ability to fulfill the requirements of the Old Covenant (because in this they have failed miserably), but because He chose to set His love upon them when He chose Abraham, Isaac, and Jacob and when He redeemed Israel as nation out of Egypt. (see Deuteronomy 4:37, 7:6-8, 9:6) In fact, Jesus came as a Jew in order to confirm the promises that God made to their ancestors. Additionally, in the very same passage where God promised the New Covenant to Old Covenant people, He promises that He will not reject Israel, even in spite of their many sins and errors.

> *Romans 15:8 - For I tell you that Christ has become a servant of the Jews on behalf of God's truth, so that the promises made to the patriarchs might be confirmed*

> *Jeremiah 31:37 - This is what the LORD says: "Only if the heavens above can be measured and the foundations of the earth below be searched out will I reject all the descendants of Israel because of all they have done,"*

As we covered in a previous chapter, under the Old Covenant, without the shedding of blood there is no forgiveness of sin and there is only one place in the world that God chose for acceptable sacrifices to be offered. The destruction of the Temple in 70 A.D., which included the demolition of the sacrificial system, confirmed that the Old Covenant Law has become obsolete as a means of obtaining right standing with God. (see Hebrews 8:13) This is because Jesus offered Himself and shed His blood for our sins in the place that God ordained for acceptable sacrifices in order to fulfill the Old Covenant and establish the New Covenant for all who believe that He is the Messiah. The coming of Messiah is a consolation to the Jews. (see Luke 2:25; Isaiah 12:1, 49:13) It is GOOD NEWS and the fulfillment of all of their hopes!

Therefore, God sustains the Jewish people by His mercy until they understand what He has done for them by sending His Son. Love is patient, and God's patience extends for thousands of years. Jews do not receive salvation just because they are Jewish, just like not every professing Christian will receive salvation just because they go to church. There is no hope for Israel apart from faith in Jesus as their Messiah. All Jews who continue to reject Jesus are just as lost as any heathen and will be eternally cut off from God's people for not listening to His Son. (see Deuteronomy 18:18-19) Paul even went so far as to call unbelieving Jews *enemies of the Gospel* because of their present hostility toward Jesus, but God still loves them because He unconditionally set his love upon their ancestors in a covenant with them which precedes the Law of Moses. (see Genesis 12:1-3, 15:1-19, 17:1-14)

> *Romans 11:28-29 - As far as the gospel is concerned, they are enemies for your sake; but as far as election is concerned, they are loved on account of the patriarchs, for God's gifts and his call are irrevocable.*

As God's adopted children, ingrafted by faith into His promises to Israel, we are called to love what God loves and join Him in His extension of mercy to the Jewish people. If God's undeserved kindness for the people who once rejected Jesus is offensive to us, then it only shows that we do not fully understand the unwarranted mercy that God has shown to us.

When Paul preached to the Jews who had not yet heard that the Messiah had come, He taught how Jesus fulfilled the Scriptures, particularly Isaiah 53 pertaining to the suffering servant of God. He pointed out the necessity of a blood sacrifice for the atonement of sin and how the Law of Moses was unable to provide complete ongoing righteousness in the sight of God. Paul warned them about the Day of the Lord spoken of by God's prophets, which is still yet to come and on which the righteous and the wicked will be judged. He made clear to them that the only way to be included with the righteous was not through the Law but only by faith in Jesus as their Messiah.

> *Acts 26:22-23 - But God has helped me to this very day; so I stand here and testify to small and great alike. I am saying nothing beyond what the prophets and Moses said would happen-- that the Messiah would suffer and, as the first to rise from the dead, would bring the message of light to his own people and to the Gentiles." (referring to Isaiah 53)*

> *Acts 13:38-41 - "Therefore, my friends, I want you to know that through Jesus the forgiveness of sins is proclaimed to you. Through him everyone who believes is set free from every sin, a justification you were not able to obtain under the law of Moses. Take care that what the prophets have said does not happen to you: " 'Look, you scoffers, wonder and perish, for I am going to do something in your days that you would never believe, even if someone told you.'" (quoting Habakkuk 1:5)*

When we pray for the Jewish people, we can agree with what the Scriptures say about God's love for them. Like Moses, Daniel, Nehemiah, and Ezra, we can pray for God to bless them on account of His great mercy and not because of anything they have done to deserve it. Truth be told, there are innumerable prophetic passages of Scripture which include promises from God for the restoration of His people, Israel. We can pray that, through the fulfillment of these Scriptures, Jews will see plainly the faithfulness of God in keeping His word to them and that through this, they gain a deeper understanding of His ways and His mercy. Additionally, as God's New Covenant priests, (see 1 Peter 2:9) we can follow Joel's instruction to pray to God to show mercy to the people of Israel, even if only on account of His own reputation in the sight of the nations.

> *Joel 2:17 - Let the priests, who minister before the LORD, weep between the portico and the altar. Let them say, "Spare your*

*people, LORD. Do not make your inheritance an object of scorn,
a byword among the nations. Why should they say among the
peoples, 'Where is their God?' "*

The aim of all of this is for Jews to come to recognize and know Jesus as
their Lord and Messiah. We can pray for God to send the Holy Spirit to
circumcise their hearts and make them true Jews who are made whole in
their Savior. (see Romans 2:28-29; Deuteronomy 30:6) Additionally, Paul
said that Jews demand a sign, so we can pray for the Lord to sovereignly
and miraculously make Himself known to them in order to confirm that
Jesus is their Messiah. (1 Corinthians 1:22)

At the same time, it is our job as believers to provoke the Jews to jealousy
because we possess what they long to have. (see Romans 11:11,13) We
have the Lord (Adonai), the Messiah who fulfills their Scriptures, gives us
hearts to obey God in purity and righteousness, and sets us apart for
God's Kingdom. We have the power of the God who parted the waters of
the Red Sea for them dwelling within us and giving us the ability to work
miracles, signs, and wonders. Because Jews are persuaded by miraculous
signs, we must be equipped to demonstrate God's power through
supernatural healing, deliverance, and speaking prophetic words to reveal
the secrets of their hearts in order to point them to Jesus as the Messiah.
Most significantly, the way we love them with supernatural mercy for
their stubborn and stiff-necked tendencies, superiority, and chronic
complaining will speak volumes to them even if we don't say a word.

Though in times past it has seemed implausible that Jews would believe
in Jesus, we live in a time when it is happening more and more. Whereas
God previously hardened Jewish hearts to the Gospel message, He did
this so that every Gentile marked for eternal life could come to know
Jesus and be saved. As the time of the Gentiles is reaching its fulfillment, a
softening of Jewish hearts to the love of God has already begun and will
continue to increase. (see Romans 11:7-10, 25; Luke 21:24) God knows
those who are His *out of every* nation, tribe, and tongue, including the
Jewish people. We can agree in prayer with the Scriptures that, in the end,
all those who are true Israelites in their hearts will be saved.

It is also good for us to pray that God gives special strength to new Jewish believers in Jesus. They very well may face hostility, persecution, rejection, and abandonment from their family, friends, and community because of their faith in Jesus as Messiah. We can also pray that God surrounds them with laborers who will be able to walk with them through the beginning phases of their faith without forcing them to give up their Jewish identity. And of course, if we are the laborer whom God chooses to send, we can love them and support them as they choose eternal life over the things of this world, and encourage them to live as a Jew who finally has an eternal King.

In addition to all of this, every believer has a good reason to pray for the Jewish people. Jesus is not coming back until Jerusalem says, "Blessed is He who comes in the name of the Lord." (see Matthew 23:39; Luke 13:35) The same people whose ancestors cried "Hosanna" in the streets as Jesus entered in as their King but then several days later rejected Him and put Him to death as a blasphemer, will one day look upon the One they have pierced and again shout "Hosanna" to receive Jesus as their Messiah. (see Hosea 3:1-5; Zechariah 12:10-13:2; Matthew 21:9) When Jesus said to His disciples, "*I am come* to fulfill the Law and the Prophets," He used a verb tense which expressed that He was there in that time and that He will come again to bring to completion everything that the Scriptures say in accordance with God's perfect and pleasing will. (see Matthew 5:17) He came the first time as the suffering servant of God and the Lamb of God who takes away the sins of the world. (see Isaiah 53; John 1:29) When He returns as the lion of Judah and the conquering King, all of God's promises to Israel of ultimate restoration and glory will be fulfilled, and we will all rejoice together. Hallelujah!

For more on this subject, read Romans 9-11, Jeremiah 31-33, Ephesians 2, Zechariah 12-13, and see also Ezekiel 20:39-44, 39:21-29.

FOR ALL PEOPLE & THE NATIONS

Paul did not give us an example of praying for Gentile unbelievers or for nations but he did write instructions to Timothy, which give us insight into his thoughts on the matter.

> *1 Timothy 2:1-6 - I urge, then, first of all, that petitions, prayers, intercession and thanksgiving be made for all people-- for kings*

and all those in authority, that we may live peaceful and quiet lives in all godliness and holiness. This is good, and pleases God our Savior, who wants all people to be saved and to come to a knowledge of the truth. For there is one God and one mediator between God and mankind, the man Christ Jesus, who gave himself as a ransom for all people. This has now been witnessed to at the proper time.

Paul started with *first of all,* but this does not mean that praying for the lost is the first and highest priority of our prayer meetings. In the context of Paul's letter to Timothy, Timothy was ministering to the church at Ephesus and some false teachers had come there teaching that it was only through special knowledge and following the Old Covenant Law that people could know God and be saved. Instead of offering the free gift of God's grace to all people through faith in Christ alone, they constructed spiritually legalistic belief systems, promoted speculation by arguing about minor details, and wanted to become famous as teachers of God's Law. (see 1 Timothy 1:3-7) Not only this, but they claimed to be the only ones with revelation of the truth and condemned everyone who did not follow their teaching with doomsday messages of God's judgment. In contrast to them, Paul pointed to his own life as the ultimate example of God's grace and mercy. Even though Paul was far more trained and qualified at teaching God's Law than any of the false teachers, he put the Law in its rightful place in order to be a walking and talking demonstration of God's endless mercy.

1 Timothy 1:13-16 - Even though I was once a blasphemer and a persecutor and a violent man, I was shown mercy because I acted in ignorance and unbelief. The grace of our Lord was poured out on me abundantly, along with the faith and love that are in Christ Jesus. Here is a trustworthy saying that deserves full acceptance: Christ Jesus came into the world to save sinners--of whom I am the worst. But for that very reason I was shown mercy so that in me, the worst of sinners, Christ Jesus might display his immense patience as an example for those who would believe in him and receive eternal life.

Paul wanted to be sure that Timothy's faith was not going to be shipwrecked by the false teachers and their teachings. Accordingly, Paul's *first of all* was to emphasize that Jesus is not *against* anyone but *for* all people. It is God's desire for everyone to be saved through faith in His Son, Jesus Christ. We are not messengers of bad news of God's judgment but Good News of the one and only way God has made for them to be set free from condemnation forever! It is the kindness of God that leads to repentance and, as such, we offer up prayers, petitions, intercession, and thanksgiving on behalf of all people. This means asking God to help them, praying for them what they do not know how to pray for themselves, talking with God about them, and listening for His perspective and insight so that we can love them well. If nothing else, we can thank God for bringing them into our lives and for the way that He is using them to draw us closer to Him. And we can ask God to bless them for it.

Paul continued by emphasizing prayer *for kings and all those who are in positions of authority.* All authority is appointed by God and we are to submit to those placed in positions of authority over us. (see Romans 13:1-7; Titus 3:1; 1 Peter 2:13-14) Significantly, Paul wrote this during a time of intense persecution against Christians which was sometimes sanctioned by the governing authorities but Paul still instructed that prayers be made *for* them, not against them in any way.

Authorities are appointed by God as agents of justice to punish the wicked and reward the good. While this does not always seem to be the case, it is also important to remember that God is not in a rush and His timetable is quite different than ours. For example, God told Abraham that his descendants would suffer harsh slavery and affliction for four hundred years because it would be unjust for Him to displace the Amorites out of their land until their sins had accumulated to a level that warranted that level of judgment. (see Genesis 15:14-16) In another example, God told Moses that He would avenge Israel by destroying the Amalekites from the face of the earth, but He did not bring about this destruction until several hundred years later during the rule of Saul, the first King of Israel. (see Exodus 17:14; 1 Samuel 15:2-3) Because of Judah's ongoing sin and leadership failures, God used Babylon, even calling Babylon's king Nebuchadnezzar His servant, to conquer His own people and even to destroy Jerusalem. (see Jeremiah 27:6, 43:10) But then later in history, God used the Persians, calling Persia's king Cyrus His anointed one, to conquer and punish the Babylonians on account of the way they had treated His people and to make a way for His people to return to their land. (see Isaiah 45:1) Needless to say, God's ways are not our ways, and He is not shortsighted or quick to wrath. More than this, God delights in showing mercy. When a nation deserving God's justice repents of their sin, He oftentimes relents and withholds warranted judgment. (see Jeremiah 2:14, 18:8, 26:13; Exodus 32:14) Even Nineveh, a city full of violence and cruelty warranting utter destruction, had a king who led the people of the city into repentance when he heard Jonah's offer of mercy. Because of this, God spared them from the destruction they deserved. (see Jonah 3:6-10) God holds the hearts of all kings and leaders in His hand to lead people higher into righteousness or deeper into sin according to His will and purposes in the earth. (see Proverbs 21:1, 14:34)

However, when we see natural or man-made catastrophes in various parts of the world, we cannot condemn those who suffer or die as a result of these disasters as if they are worse sinners than any of us. There is no use in going on research expeditions to discover the sins in various cultures or parts of the world that may seem to have warranted hardships or divine punishment. (see Luke 13:1-5) Everyone in every nation falls equally short of God's perfect standard and deserves the wrath of God. And yet, it is still God's desire for everyone to be saved. We must never forget that our job as New Covenant ministers of reconciliation is to *not hold* people's sins against them but instead to extend the mercy of God to all people through faith in Jesus Christ. (see 1 Corinthians 5:18-19) Therefore, no matter what disasters may happen all over the world, the only issue deserving our attention now is proclaiming the Gospel.

The reason Paul gave for praying for all people and those in authority was so that believers could live *peaceful and quiet lives in all godliness and holiness.* He wanted believers to be free to live their lives for the Lord with as few hindrances and disturbances as possible. If neighbors, cities, or nations are hostile toward the Christian faith, it creates obstacles to personal piety and makes it more challenging to honor God in our words, actions, and to spread the Good News. In some translations, the word for *holiness* in this passage is translated as *honesty*. If the governing authorities make it illegal to worship Jesus or require those under their authority to do things that are against God's ways, then believers have a crisis of integrity. It was Paul's preference for worshiping Jesus to remain a matter of eternal life or death so that believers would not be confronted with the issue of literally living or dying due to persecution and martyrdom for Christ. Additionally, lack of persecution and antagonism makes it much easier for God's laborers to do His work.

Paul also desired for prayer for all people to be without anger or doubt in God's mercy and good will toward all men.

> *1 Timothy 2:8 - Therefore I want the men everywhere to pray, lifting up holy hands without anger or disputing.*

When we pray for the lost (or for anyone for that matter), we must do so from a heart of genuine love for them. Angry prayers are not from the heart of God who loved the world so much that He gave His Son not to judge but to save everyone who would believe. (see John 3:16-17) If we find ourselves praying with anger, which is typically a result of our own fear or self-righteousness, then it is best not to pray for the person until the Lord has changed our heart toward them. If for any reason we dispute in our minds about God's desire or ability to show mercy or to bless them, then we probably lack understanding of the extent of God's grace in our own lives. It is a good practice to pray for others only what we would want someone else to pray for us. Or, better yet, pray the way we would want Jesus to pray for us. The best prayers are led by the Holy Spirit in the will of God and flow from a heart of unfeigned compassion.

Paul also mentioned prayer in the posture of *lifting up holy hands*. While there are many and varied explanations for this posture, the first reference in the Scriptures of man reaching out his hand is when God blocked the way to the tree of life with a flaming sword and cherubim so that fallen man would not have access to eternal life. (see Genesis 3:22-24) Everything God has done since Adam's wrong choice in the Garden of Eden has been for the purpose of encouraging us to reach out to Him and to make a way for us to eat of the tree of life again. This culminated in Jesus Christ, who is the way God has made for our access to Him to be restored. (see John 14:6; Romans 5:2) When we lift up our hands to God through faith in Jesus, we reach out to the Creator of the Universe to partake of the eternal tree of life and to restore paradise to earth – as it is in heaven.

When Paul proclaimed the Gospel to Gentile unbelievers, he emphasized God's power as Creator of the Universe and desire for all people to search for Him and reach out to find Him. This meant that they would need to turn from the gods and priorities of this world and from idolizing people as gods (even Paul and his traveling companions) in order to worship the one true God, who is sovereign over all nations.

> *Acts 14:15-17 - "Friends, why are you doing this? We too are only human, like you. We are bringing you good news, telling you to turn from these worthless things to the living God, who made the heavens and the earth and the sea and everything in them. In the past, he let all nations go their own way. Yet he has not left himself without testimony: He has shown kindness by giving you rain from heaven and crops in their seasons; he provides you with plenty of food and fills your hearts with joy."*

> *Acts 17:26-31 - From one man he made all the nations, that they should inhabit the whole earth; and he marked out their appointed times in history and the boundaries of their lands. God did this so that they would seek him and perhaps reach out for him and find him, though he is not far from any one of us. 'For in him we live and move and have our being.' As some of your own poets have said, 'We are his offspring.' "Therefore since we are God's offspring, we should not think that the divine being is like gold or silver or stone--an image made by human design and skill. In the past God overlooked such ignorance, but now he commands all people everywhere to repent. For he has set a day when he will judge the world with justice by the man he has appointed. He has given proof of this to everyone by raising him from the dead."*

When we pray for Gentile unbelievers, we can pray for them to come to know Jesus for themselves. Only God knows how to bring this about in each person's life. Paul said that Gentiles look for wisdom. (see 1 Corinthians 1:22) Sometimes, this means wisdom that will give them a better life, and other times this means intelligence that is beyond their scope of comprehension. So, while we are praying for them, it is important that we live our lives by the guidance and purity of the Holy Spirit so that we reveal God's power, faithfulness, and holiness through our choices and actions. Even in the midst of our most difficult trials in life, we must be uncompromising in our faith and trust in Jesus and His sufficiency. We must reveal true love to them by being patient with them and by overlooking their vanity, impatience, tendency toward arrogance, and constant chasing after every new scheme for success. We have been placed in the lives of unbelievers among all of the nations not only to pray for them but also to reveal to them what true success is— righteousness, peace, and joy in the Holy Spirit. It is Heaven on earth.

As far as unbelieving nations are concerned, there is no Biblical example of prayer for them. Rather, there are innumerable references in the Scriptures about God moving in power on behalf of His people when they trust Him to protect, defend, and bless them so that all nations of the earth can see plainly that He is the one, true, all-powerful God. The only possible exception to this is the prophetic words uttered by God's Prophets, though I consider this to be a different form of prayer altogether. Even so, the prophets prophesied God's declarations to the nations regarding their rise and fall based on their treatment of God's people and their participation in sins which cause nations to warrant destruction. (see Leviticus 18:24-28; Deuteronomy 18:9-14) Besides the church and the people of Israel/the Jews, there is no nation on earth that has a covenant relationship with God. And even so, without faith in Jesus, everyone and every nation is equally deserving of judgment. The only thing left to pray for is God's mercy and for the righteous to do their job in proclaiming the Good News of salvation so that all who believe in Jesus will be spared from the wrath to come.

In the end, all (yes, all) nations of the earth will gather together to conspire against God and war against Jerusalem. Followers of Christ will be hated by everyone in the world because of our faith in Jesus. (see

Zechariah 12:3, 14:2; Joel 3:2; Matthew 10:22) But, God will come to the defense of everyone who calls upon the name of the Lord and we have no need of fearing those who cannot touch our soul. As God's children and Christ's followers, we demonstrate our testimony of His position in our lives by not denying Him and by enduring through hostility and persecution until He comes to rescue us from this world forever. (see Revelation 13:7-10, 14:12) Then, He will gather all the nations together and judge between those who have known Him and those who have not, as revealed by how they treated those who have faithfully followed Him. (see Matthew 25:31-46; Mark 3:34)

For more wisdom about the nations, see Psalms 2, 9, 33, 46 & 47, 66 & 67, 79, 83, 96-100, 114 & 115, and 117.

I WOULD TO GOD

As laborers in the world, our responsibility and assignment while we are still on this earth is to share the Good News with unbelievers and to pray for them to come to trust in Jesus as their Lord, Savior, and Messiah. This said, we cannot doubt God's fairness in judging those who are given the opportunity, or even multiple opportunities, to trust in Jesus for salvation and reject the offer of God's grace.

Jesus went into various cities proclaiming the Gospel and working miracles, signs, and wonders to demonstrate the reality of the Kingdom of Heaven and the truth of His message. But when cities that had heard and seen the Gospel and its power rejected Jesus and His message, He pronounced *woe* to them as a declaration of judgment against them. (see Matthew 11:20-24) However, He did not defend Himself or retaliate in any way but instead entrusted Himself into His Father's hands. Similarly, when Jesus sent His disciples out to proclaim the Gospel and work miracles in His name, He instructed them to *shake the dust off of their feet* from any place that did not receive them and their message. This is an act of separation that calls for God's judgment against those who rejected them on account of the Gospel. But, Jesus strictly prohibited His disciples from avenging themselves or bringing about judgment upon those who were unwelcoming. (see Luke 9:55; Romans 12:19) Only God knows people's hearts, and it is always His desire for even the worst of sinners to come into knowledge of the truth and be saved. Vengeance and justice are always best left in God's hands and He is always perfectly just. We can never forget that while Jesus was being crucified by Jews and Gentiles alike, He cried out, "Father, forgive them for they know not what they do." (see Luke 23:43)

Therefore, no matter how bitterly opposed we may be by unbelievers, Jew or Gentile, we must strive to maintain our hearts in absolute mercy toward them so that we are ready to make the most of every opportunity God gives us to share our Christian faith with them. For example, Paul stood before king Agrippa as a prisoner in shackles on trial due to false accusations that had been stirred up against him because he proclaimed the Gospel of Jesus Christ. Paul did not plead for his own release or comfort but instead shared the story of his faith in Jesus. They had this exchange:

> Acts 26:28-29 NKJV - Then Agrippa said to Paul, "You almost persuade me to become a Christian." And Paul said, "I would to God that not only you, but also all who hear me today, might become both almost and altogether such as I am, except for these chains."

Paul's words, *I would to God*, do not have an English equivalent. In effect, he said, "By some extraordinary set of unexplainable and unexpected circumstances which only God could bring about, I wish that everyone in the world could be saved." At this point in Paul's life, he had been opposed, persecuted, beaten, imprisoned, and had even shaken the dust off of his feet in several cities where they rejected Jesus as the Messiah. Nevertheless, even though he knew it would not be a reality for everyone in the world to be saved, the condition of his heart remained as one full of love that always hopes.

May our hearts become like Jesus and Paul who gave their lives for the sake of the chosen. And may we always remain hopeful with our own sincere *would to God* that all people could know the love of Jesus.

CHAPTER SEVEN
GLORY TO GOD

WE NOW HAVE THIS LIGHT SHINING IN OUR
HEARTS, BUT WE OURSELVES ARE LIKE FRAGILE CLAY
JARS CONTAINING THIS GREAT TREASURE. THIS
MAKES IT CLEAR THAT OUR GREAT POWER IS FROM
GOD, NOT FROM OURSELVES.
– THE APOSTLE PAUL, 2 CORINTHIANS 4:7 NLT

The Apostle Paul was not ashamed to give God glory in everything he did, and he lived his life for the glory of God. Although this may sound expected and simple enough, the issue of who is worthy of glory has actually been the chief controversy since the beginning of creation.

As we discussed in a previous chapter, *glory* has to do with *weight, substance, wealth,* and *honor* and can also pertain to a *state of exaltation or majesty.* When we *give glory* to someone, we *keep them in a good reputation* in our own hearts and before others.

In a category by Himself, God's glory includes His status as the one and only all-powerful Creator of the whole Universe, the owner of everything, and the fact that He maintains a majestic heavenly position of highest authority over all things. In recognition of this, the heavenly host constantly worship around the throne of God, rightly identifying Him as the only one worthy of all praise.

Revelation 4:10-11 - the twenty-four elders fall down before him who sits on the throne and worship him who lives for ever and ever. They lay their crowns before the throne and say: "You are worthy, our Lord and God, to receive glory and honor and power, for you created all things, and by your will they were created and have their being."

Revelation 5:11-12 - Then I looked and heard the voice of many angels, numbering thousands upon thousands, and ten thousand times ten thousand. They encircled the throne and the living creatures and the elders. In a loud voice they were saying: "Worthy is the Lamb, who was slain, to receive power and wealth and wisdom and strength and honor and glory and praise!"

God reveals and has revealed His glory on the earth in many and various ways. Some examples include the fact that all of creation holds God in a good reputation through a vivid and intricate display of His grandness as Creator while also groaning in longing for the day when God's original design for creation will be restored. (see Psalm 19:1; Romans 8:20-22) God displayed His power and presence, also known as *Shekinah*, to Israel when He led them with a supernatural pillar of fire and a cloud of smoke, appeared as a consuming fire over Mount Sinai, filled the Tabernacle with a thick cloud, and hovered over it with fire. (see Exodus 13:21, 19:18, 40:34, 38) God demonstrated His wealth and capability as provider for His people when He sent a superabundance of quail at their fingertips to keep their bellies full in addition to manna for forty years. (see Exodus 16:7, 35) At the dedication of Solomon's Temple, God's glorious presence was so thick and weighty that the priests were unable to stand upright to minister. (see 1 Kings 8:10-12; 2 Chronicles 5:14, 7:2) When God's people trusted Him to do so, His sovereignty over nations was proven as He defended and protected them from enemies much stronger and more powerful than they were. Most significantly, God revealed His glory in His Son, Jesus Christ, who is the exact representation of God's good nature and authority over all creation. Jesus demonstrated God's power and goodness by healing the sick, casting out demons, raising the dead, and even commanding the weather. He emanated so much of God's Shekinah, even while in the flesh, that the strongest soldiers in the world could not stand on their feet in His presence. (see Hebrews 1:3; John 18:6)

However, not everyone has considered it worthwhile to give glory to God. For example, in spite of experiencing the majesty of worshiping God in the heavenly realms, satan sought glory for himself. While he at one time had been the chief worship leader in all creation, it was not enough for him. Pride and beauty corrupted his heart, and he desired God's position of authority. While he strategized a hostile takeover of God's throne to exalt himself, he defiled the sanctuary of God with merchandising and violence. (see Isaiah 14:12-15; Ezekiel 28:13-19) Later, Adam also sought glory for himself rather than trusting God and holding Him in good reputation. The one whom God had made in His likeness and to whom God had delegated all authority over creation was deceived into believing that God was cruelly withholding something from him that he needed in order to be like God. Adam disobeyed God's instructions and ate from the wrong tree seeking to obtain special knowledge that would elevate his status. (see Genesis 3) As the course of humanity continued, people forgot and disregarded God's position as Creator and began to worship created things or people and sought spirituality apart from God that would enable them to indulge all of their desires and lusts. (see Romans 1:18-20) Even today, some people, like those who built the tower of Babel, work tirelessly in attempts to make a name for themselves and to reach such a high status that they no longer need God for anything. (see Genesis 11:1-9) Others, like king Herod, have been able to elevate themselves to high positions but then become so arrogant that they consider themselves to be a god and receive worship from other people for their own persuasiveness and power rather than acknowledging God. (see Acts 12:21-23)

Not glorifying God or acknowledging His position of incomparable preeminence can seem like a small thing, but it can have eternal ramifications. All rebellion against God is the same as eating from the wrong tree in pursuit of knowledge that will help us to manipulate a desired outcome using a power other than God's. Insubordination to God is high treason against the Creator of the Universe, arrogantly puffing ourselves up to His level which is the same as idolatry. (see 1 Samuel 15:23) Unfortunately for them, rebels of the past have suffered the consequences. Satan was cast out of God's presence and thrown down to the place of the dead. Adam and his wife were banished from paradise and they, along with all creation, were placed under a curse. The builders of the Tower of Babel were scattered and sent into utter confusion. Herod was publicly eaten by worms for allowing himself to receive glory from the crowd who worshipped him as a god. Eternally speaking, all who do not submit themselves to God by acknowledging His rightful position of sovereignty over all things will be banished to eternal darkness where there is weeping, gnashing of teeth, and the flesh eating worms do not tire out.

In contrast, Jesus submitted Himself entirely to God and obeyed Him in all things. Although He was equal in sovereignty with God, He did not make an idol of Himself but, rather, sought only to do what His Father sent Him to do and brought glory to God by completing the work God had given Him to do. (see Philippians 2:6-8; John 12:26, 17:1, 4; Revelation 13:8) His judgment in all situations was fair and justified because He did not selfishly seek His own benefit but only to do God's will. (see John 5:30) When the time came for Him to offer up His life, His resounding cry was simply, "Father, glorify Your name!" because He trusted in God's good nature and knew that God would not withhold anything good from Him.

Obedience also has eternal consequences. Instead of abandoning Jesus to the grave, God raised Jesus from the dead and seated Him at His right hand for all eternity just as He had promised.

Philippians 2:9-11 - Therefore God exalted him to the highest place and gave him the name that is above every name, that at the name of Jesus every knee should bow, in heaven and on earth and under the earth, and every tongue acknowledge that Jesus Christ is Lord, to the glory of God the Father.

Because Jesus trusted in His Father's good reputation and ability to fulfill His word, even when it came to overpowering death, God honored Jesus by giving Him all things and all authority. Even so, Jesus is not quite done giving glory to His Father. At the end of the age, after death and the grave have been banished forever, Jesus will give the Kingdom back to His Father as the ultimate acknowledgment of God's rightful place as Sovereign Creator over all. (see John 3:35, 17:1, 10; 1 Corinthians 15:24, 27)

In the meantime, we give weight to who God is and what He has done for us by believing Jesus. God is love. God revealed His love to us by sending His Son, Jesus, to die for our sins, mistakes, and errors which were preventing us from having access to Him and receiving His richest blessings. All other gods demand to be served so that they can be exalted, but our God lowered Himself to serve us so that we could be lifted up. All other lords seek to amass treasures to make themselves great, but our Lord became poor so that we could be blessed with every blessing. We accurately represent our loving Heavenly Father and His character when we accept and believe that Jesus did this for us.

Moreover, our obedience glorifies God because it reveals that we love Him and value Him for who He truly is. We glorify God when we obey Him, allow Him to work His nature in us, and follow the promptings of the Holy Spirit as a lifestyle intent on fulfilling God's purposes. When we obey Him, our actions come into alignment with the chorus of heaven, silently shouting that we truly believe that God is worthy of *our* power, *our* wealth, *our* strength, *our* honor, and *our* praise. There is no pride in genuine obedience because we know that we are merely doing what God has placed in our hearts to do and that His ways are beyond what we are capable of conceiving for ourselves or bringing about in our own strength. Even when the time comes for us to receive our eternal rewards, we will know that we do not deserve them because we were only doing our duty. (see Luke 17:10) We will cast all of our rewards at the feet of our God and our King because He is the one who deserves them. (see Revelation 4:10)

The Apostle Paul understood the ramifications of both sides of the *who-deserves-the-glory* debate and what a marvelous thing God has done for us by giving His Son. God has leveled the playing field for all mankind because everyone falls short of God's perfect standard. But, all who give glory to God through faith in Jesus will rejoice together and worship God along with the heavenly host for all eternity.

> *Romans 11:33-36 - Oh, the depth of the riches of the wisdom and knowledge of God! How unsearchable his judgments, and his paths beyond tracing out! "Who has known the mind of the Lord? Or who has been his counselor?" "Who has ever given to God, that God should repay them?" For from him and through*

him and for him are all things. To him be the glory forever! Amen.

The primary purpose of most of Paul's prayers was for us to give glory to God in every aspect of our lives by allowing Him to have His way in us and to replace our heart of stone with His Holy Spirit. Actually, Paul's passion in glorifying God often results in long-winded passages of Scripture so, as we move through this chapter, I encourage you to take your time while you read and allow his exuberance to penetrate into your heart.

GIVE GLORY TO GOD

Paul, being Jewish, knew that the phrase *give glory to God* is a Hebrew idiom for confessing our sins or vowing to tell the whole truth and nothing but the truth. For example, when a blind man received his sight from Jesus, religious leaders demanded that he give *glory to God* as their way of saying, *confess that you are a liar* or *start telling the truth.* (see John 9:24) Because they did not believe that Jesus was God in the flesh, they did not understand that the healed man *was* giving glory to God by praising Jesus for healing Him or that he *was* telling them the truth. Without further debate and a little frustration that they did not believe him, the healed man shared his simple testimony that he had been blind but now he could see and pointed to this as proof that Jesus must have been sent by God.

Similarly, we give glory to God in the Christian life by confessing our sinful state and telling the truth that, without Jesus, we are wretched and hopeless. In this, we fully acknowledge to the depth of our being that we are what we are only because of God's mercy and grace toward us and not because of anything we have done to deserve it.

On several occasions in his letters, the Apostle Paul expounded on glorifying God based on what Jesus has done for us. This is what Paul said:

Galatians 1:3-5 - Grace and peace to you from God our Father and the Lord Jesus Christ, who gave himself for our sins to rescue us from the present evil age, according to the will of our God and Father, to whom be glory for ever and ever. Amen.

1 Timothy 1:15-17 - Here is a trustworthy saying that deserves full acceptance: Christ Jesus came into the world to save sinners--of whom I am the worst. But for that very reason I was shown mercy so that in me, the worst of sinners, Christ Jesus might display his immense patience as an example for those who would believe in him and receive eternal life. Now to the King eternal, immortal, invisible, the only God, be honor and glory for ever and ever. Amen.

Romans 5:1-2 - Therefore, since we have been justified through faith, we have peace with God through our Lord Jesus Christ, through whom we have gained access by faith into this grace in which we now stand. And we boast in the hope of the glory of God.

When we testify truthfully about what God has done in our lives and that, in our own way, we were once blind but now we see, we give weight to what Jesus has done for us and hold God in a good reputation as the only One who is able to save. We have been called to know God, to believe Him, and to be His witnesses in the earth who testify of His faithfulness not because of anything that we have done but entirely because of His sovereignty, goodness, and love. We have been chosen by God for the singular purpose of bringing Him glory. (see Isaiah 43:7) We have been adopted as God's children and redeemed from Adam's mistake by the One who crushed the head of the ancient serpent to show His power over all things for the rest of eternity. When we deserved wrath, He showed us mercy and He continues to show us mercy each and every day. More than this, He has marked us and sealed us with the guarantee of the Holy Spirit so that we can look forward with confident expectation to all that is to come. Paul put it this way:

Ephesians 1:12-14 NLT - God's purpose was that we Jews who were the first to trust in Christ would bring praise and glory to God. And now you Gentiles have also heard the truth, the Good News that God saves you. And when you believed in Christ, he identified you as his own by giving you the Holy Spirit, whom he promised long ago. The Spirit is God's guarantee that he will give us the inheritance he promised and that he has purchased us to be his own people. He did this so we would praise and glorify him.

Romans 16:25-27 - Now to him who is able to establish you in accordance with my gospel, the message I proclaim about Jesus Christ, in keeping with the revelation of the mystery hidden for long ages past, but now revealed and made known through the prophetic writings by the command of the eternal God, so that all the Gentiles might come to the obedience that comes from faith-- to the only wise God be glory forever through Jesus Christ! Amen.

Romans 9:23 - What if he did this to make the riches of his glory known to the objects of his mercy, whom he prepared in advance for glory—

As we live to give glory to God, let there be no question in our hearts that He is truly the one worthy of it all.

LIVING TO GLORIFY GOD

Paul exhorted believers to live lives of purity in order to demonstrate God's goodness and holiness plainly for all to see. Like Jesus, who gave glory to God by adhering to God's ways without giving way to sin, God's love for us enables us to stop doing things our own way for our own selfish reasons. His heart becomes our heart and we stop judging others or trying to be superior for any reason. It becomes our genuine desire to please God in every way and to refute anything that stands or speaks against His good reputation.

Romans 15:7 NLT - Therefore, accept each other just as Christ has accepted you so that God will be given glory.

1 Corinthians 10:31 - So whether you eat or drink or whatever you do, do it all for the glory of God.

1 Corinthians 6:20 KJV - For ye are bought with a price: therefore glorify God in your body, and in your spirit, which are God's.

Philippians 1:11 NLT - May you always be filled with the fruit of your salvation--the righteous character produced in your life by

Jesus Christ--for this will bring much glory and praise to God.

1 Timothy 1:9-11 - We also know that the law is made not for the righteous but for lawbreakers and rebels, the ungodly and sinful, the unholy and irreligious, for those who kill their fathers or mothers, for murderers, for the sexually immoral, for those practicing homosexuality, for slave traders and liars and perjurers--and for whatever else is contrary to the sound doctrine that conforms to the gospel concerning the glory of the blessed God, which he entrusted to me.

When we keep our sights on our eternal destination and live lives of integrity, purity, and righteousness, we demonstrate that we believe that living to glorify God was more important than temporal matters. Paul exhibited this in his own life and he invited all believers to join with him in following the faithful ones who showed us how to trust God even in seemingly impossible circumstances. The heroes from Hebrews Chapter 11, commonly called the "Hall of Faith," give us examples of unswerving devotion to God and His ways because they would not be deterred away from believing God's goodness and faithfulness. For example, Abraham gave glory to God by not wavering away from believing that God had power and was able to do what He had promised by giving Abraham and Sarah a son even though Abraham was almost 100 years old and Sarah was way past the age of child-bearing. Moses chose to share in the oppression of God's people by being known as a Hebrew when he could have chosen to stay in Pharaoh's palace and enjoy the splendors of Egypt. He did this because he considered God's value to be greater than all the riches in the world. Jesus believed that the eternal rewards that God had promised Him were worth more than life itself. So, He trusted in God's power over death and the grave, and also trusted in God's ability to faithfully fulfill His word. All of these people, and many others, are the witnesses who testify of God's faithfulness to those who trust in Him.

Therefore, no matter what we encounter, their testimonies give us an example to follow so that we can live our lives for God's purposes and trust Him with our lives no matter what happens. Actually, sometimes it seems like the worse the scenario becomes from a human perspective, the more glory God receives. Somehow, I think He likes it that way. This is because when we stand in faith, we demonstrate that our strength comes from Him and that we consider Him to be more precious and valuable than anything this life has to offer.

Romans 8:18 - I consider that our present sufferings are not worth comparing with the glory that will be revealed in us.

1 Timothy 6:13-16 - In the sight of God, who gives life to everything, and of Christ Jesus, who while testifying before Pontius Pilate made the good confession, I charge you to keep this command without spot or blame until the appearing of our Lord Jesus Christ, which God will bring about in his own time-- God, the blessed and only Ruler, the King of kings and Lord of lords, who alone is immortal and who lives in unapproachable light, whom no one has seen or can see. To him be honor and might forever. Amen.

2 Corinthians 4:6-10, 15 NLT - For God, who said, "Let there be light in the darkness," has made this light shine in our hearts so we could know the glory of God that is seen in the face of Jesus Christ. We now have this light shining in our hearts, but we ourselves are like fragile clay jars containing this great treasure. This makes it clear that our great power is from God, not from ourselves. We are pressed on every side by troubles, but we are not crushed. We are perplexed, but not driven to despair. We are hunted down, but never abandoned by God. We get knocked down, but we are not destroyed. Through suffering, our bodies continue to share in the death of Jesus so that the life of Jesus may also be seen in our bodies. ... All of this is for your benefit. And as God's grace reaches more and more people, there will be great thanksgiving, and God will receive more and more glory.

Fortunately, God is the one who reveals Himself to us, gives us hearts to love Him and faith to trust in Jesus no matter what happens. While we endure through trials and hardships, it is God who comforts us and gives us strength to do things His way and to stand to the end.

2 Corinthians 1:3-4 - Praise be to the God and Father of our Lord Jesus Christ, the Father of compassion and the God of all comfort, who comforts us in all our troubles, so that we can comfort those in any trouble with the comfort we ourselves receive from God.

The more we live to glorify God, the more we understand God's kindness toward us and the more we become vessels of grace, mercy, and compassion.

TRANSFORMED TO SHARE IN GLORY

In all of Paul's prayers, he knew that God's desire was for us as His children to share in His glory by being transformed into the likeness of His Son. The more we are changed in our inmost being and in our actions to be like Jesus, the more we reveal God's goodness. Our old nature was selfish and unloving but, as we understand God's great love for us, He works His love into our hearts until we personify His love. Our old self was foolish and we were, as the Scriptures call some, *worthless fellows*, but our new self is designed to reveal the great worthiness of God as we are transformed into his children as people of integrity, honor, and purity. He has chosen us, changes us by His power within us, and allows us to share more and more in His glory. Paul spoke of it this way:

Romans 8:29-30 - For those God foreknew he also predestined to be conformed to the image of his Son, that he might be the firstborn among many brothers and sisters. And those he predestined, he also called; those he called, he also justified; those he justified, he also glorified.

Ephesians 3:20-21 - Now to him who is able to do immeasurably more than all we ask or imagine, according to his power that is at work within us, to him be glory in the church and in Christ Jesus throughout all generations, for ever and ever! Amen.

2 Corinthians 3:18 - And we all, who with unveiled faces contemplate the Lord's glory, are being transformed into his image with ever-increasing glory, which comes from the Lord, who is the Spirit.

God does not share His glory with any other god, with any idol, with any government, or with any person in their own strength, but He does share it with us as His children. We share in the glory of our Father who is the Most High God and Creator of the Universe so that we can reveal His glory to others. To give an illustration from the Old Testament, Joseph wanted his father, Jacob, to see the glory that God had given him. (see Genesis 45:13) Joseph was referring to his high position of authority, second only to Pharaoh who was the most powerful man in the world in that day, and to the great wealth and abundance that God had provided in spite of famine throughout the rest of world at that time. Comparably, God has given us glory by raising us up and seating us at His right hand in Christ with all authority bestowed to us for His purposes. He enables us to bring the splendor of Heaven to earth through miracles, signs, and wonders like Jesus who first revealed His own glory as God's Son when He turned water into wine at the wedding feast in Cana. (see John 2:11) We also partake of our Father's fathomless wealth as the owner of all Creation. This does not mean that we will all live lives of luxury from the world's point of view, but it does mean that we have absolutely no need to worry about money or whether or not our Heavenly Father is willing and able to provide for all of our needs as we fulfill His purposes. (see also Matthew 6:33) Moreover, God gives us supernatural strength in our inmost being to remain faithful to Him and His ways when those without His power would crumble. And sometimes, He intervenes on our behalf to deliver us from evil in ways that only He can. In all of these things, God's reputation as our Father is on the line, and He is ready to back us up for the rest of eternity.

2 Thessalonians 2:14 - He called you to this through our gospel, that you might share in the glory of our Lord Jesus Christ.

2 Corinthians 1:20 - For no matter how many promises God has made, they are "Yes" in Christ. And so through him the "Amen" is spoken by us to the glory of God.

Philippians 4:19-20 - And my God will meet all your needs according to the riches of his glory in Christ Jesus. To our God and Father be glory for ever and ever. Amen.

Ephesians 3:16 - I pray that out of his glorious riches he may strengthen you with power through his Spirit in your inner being,

2 Timothy 4:18 - The Lord will rescue me from every evil attack and will bring me safely to his heavenly kingdom. To him be glory for ever and ever. Amen.

The more we accept and walk in the glory that God gives us freely as His children, the more we radiate His *Shekinah* just like Jesus did. Peter exuded so much of God's power that people were healed even by his shadow. (see Acts 15:5) God worked notable and unusual miracles by the hands of Paul and many were healed by the power of God just by touching handkerchiefs that he had blessed. (see 19:11-12) The church that we read about in the Book of Acts was full of miracles, signs, and wonders worked by ordinary people just like you and me. Imagine how palpable the presence and power of God must have been in their meetings!

On a side note, it is interesting to me that the same word for God's *power* can be used as the word for *virtue.* While most people want to emanate the power of God, few are willing to submit themselves to God's transformation process enough to genuinely display His perfect virtue. However, I believe that God is most glorified when His power and virtue are entwined together and displayed in harmony with one another. Only then do we accurately represent Him and keep Him in the correct and good reputation with everyone we meet.

THE GLORY TO COME

Paul knew that God gave His Son for our redemption and, ultimately, our glorification. We already spiritually dwell in a heavenly place where there is no death, mourning, sickness, crying, or pain. Soon, our literal experience will match with our spiritual condition. (see 1 Corinthians 15:43; Revelation 21:3-5) Jesus, who descended from Heaven, lived in flesh like ours, was crucified, died, was buried, and raised again, ascended back to Heaven, and is seated at the right hand of the Father as proof of God's ability to keep His word. This means that we can have absolute confidence that God will fulfill His eternal promises to us. Jesus is coming back to complete our glorification, to give us imperishable resurrection bodies, dominion over all the earth, and to dwell among us as our King.

Hallelujah!

Until then, because God **is** love, the only way to accurately keep Him in good reputation for the world to see is to love the way that He does. The aim of our life is to love like Jesus. If we know what God has done for us, we know that God loves us. If we know that God loves us, we love Him. If we love Him, we keep Jesus' commands. (see John 14:15, 23) If we keep His commands, we lay down our lives in self-sacrificing love like Jesus did. In fact, until we worship God in heaven and on the new earth, we worship Him by offering up our lives for His Kingdom and purposes. (see Romans 12:1) We cast aside our own plans, desires, ideas, preferences, and opinions in order to be led by the Holy Spirit into the plans God has for us and the good works that He has prepared for us to do. We prove through our words, actions, and our very lives that God is worthy of all that we have and all that we are. We fearlessly follow our crucified King because we know that God has given Him the greatest reward of all and that, in the same way, even when we suffer for righteousness sake and the sake of the Gospel, it only serves to increase our eternal reward.

> *2 Corinthians 4:17 - For our light and momentary troubles are achieving for us an eternal glory that far outweighs them all.*

Someday soon, we will join the host of heaven along with all of creation and shout the praises to our glorious Lord, Savior, Messiah, and King.

> *Revelation 5:13 - Then I heard every creature in heaven and on earth and under the earth and on the sea, and all that is in them, saying: "To him who sits on the throne and to the Lamb be praise and honor and glory and power, for ever and ever!"*

To God be the glory forever and ever! Amen.

ABOUT THE AUTHOR

Wendy Bowen was the ultimate Type A, workaholic, overachiever, and control-freak until she had a dramatic encounter with the Lord Jesus Christ. Since then, the Lord called Wendy to give away all of her possessions and live by faith, prayer, and obedience to His voice. She lives for the purpose of proclaiming the Gospel and building up the Church by teaching the Word of God, helping believers experience Jesus through the Holy Spirit, and equipping disciples in their Kingdom purpose. The Lord blesses her ministry with His manifest presence and with miracles, signs, and wonders.

www.activatedchurch.com

www.manifestinternational.com

www.ingramcontent.com/pod-product-compliance
Lightning Source LLC
LaVergne TN
LVHW021345080426
835508LV00020B/2114